holiday microwave ideas

microwave cooking library®

by barbara methven

microwave cooking library®

The microwave oven really proves its worth during the busy season. Speedy cooking and easy cleanup reduce time-consuming, messy jobs, and let you focus on the creative and fun aspects of holiday preparation.

This mostly microwave cookbook provides timesaving recipes for traditional favorites as well as a wealth of innovative ideas for decorating, gift-giving and entertaining. Using your microwave oven effectively does not mean using it exclusively. Sometimes the most efficient way to prepare a meal for a sizable group is to roast a large cut of meat conventionally while you microwave side dishes and reheat items made in advance. Many of the microwave recipes include make-ahead directions. In addition, this book offers conventional directions, where they are appropriate. You'll find that, using this book and your microwave oven, you can accomplish your holiday tasks in a more relaxed fashion and have leisure to enjoy the festivities, too.

Barbara Methven

CREDITS:
Design & Production: Cy DeCosse Incorporated
Senior Art Director: Rebecca Gammelgaard
Art Directors: Oksana Haliw, David Schelitzche
Project Managers: Melissa Erickson, Lynette Reber, Ann Schlachter
Home Economists: Peggy Ramette, Ann Stuart, Kathy Weber, Grace Wells
Consultants: Diana Hansen, Sally Sendmeyer, Carol Trench, Grace Wells
Recipe Editor: Janice Cauley, Susan Meyers
Production Manager: Jim Bindas
Assistant Production Managers: Julie Churchill, Jacquie Marx
Typesetting: Linda Schloegel, Jennie Smith
Production Staff: Russell Beaver, Holly Clements, Sheila DiPaola, Joe Fahey, Carol Ann Kevan, Yelena Konrardy, Cindy Natvig, Greg Wallace, Nik Wogstad
Studio Manager: Cathleen Shannon
Photographers: Rex Irmen, Tony Kubat, John Lauenstein, Bill Lindner, Mark Macemon, Mette Nielsen, Rebecca Hawthorne
Food Stylists: Melinda Hutchison, Amy Peterson, Peggy Ramette, Sue Sinon, Ann Stuart, Suzanne Finley, Robin Krause, Susan Zechman
Color Separations: Spectrum, Inc.
Printing: R. R. Donnelley & Sons (0988)

CY DE COSSE INCORPORATED
Chairman: Cy DeCosse
President: James B. Maus
Executive Vice President: William B. Jones

Library of Congress Cataloging-in-Publication Data.

Methven, Barbara.
  Holiday microwave ideas/by Barbara Methven.

  p. cm. -- (Microwave cooking library)

Includes index.
ISBN 0-86573-557-3.   ISBN 0-86573-558-1 (pbk.)
1. Microwave cookery. 2. Holiday cookery. 3. Holiday decorations.
I. Title. II. Series.
TX832.M3935   1988
641.5'68--dc19   88-9561
                                                                      CIP

Contents

What You Need to Know Before You Start

The holiday season may be your busiest time of the year, but it needn't be hectic. How can you give an important holiday party, make personal gifts for special friends, decorate your home, produce a memorable holiday dinner and still find time to join in family activities, finish your shopping and wrap the gifts? *Holiday Microwave Ideas* can help you prepare for the holidays with time to enjoy them, too. This book provides microwave shortcuts to traditional holiday fare, ideas for entertaining, and lively ways to use your imagination and the microwave oven to create gifts, goodies and decorations.

Holiday Dinner Menus

Start with the meat when planning your holiday meals. This section offers eight menus, nine popular cuts of meat and fourteen ways to prepare them.

You'll find both microwave and conventional directions for cooking the meats. For a small gathering, you may prefer to microwave the meat. When you're cooking for a crowd, the most efficient plan will be to roast the meat conventionally while you microwave an impressive array of trimmings. We recommend conventional cooking for a goose, large turkey or crown roast of pork. To shorten cooking time, roast them unstuffed and microwave the dressing.

Each menu suggests side dishes that complement the meat. To suit your own taste, convenience or family preferences, you may substitute or add other dishes from the trimmings section.

Holiday Dinner Trimmings

Every family has favorite holiday side dishes. Without them, the meal just wouldn't be complete. Here are many of your favorites updated with timesaving microwave techniques. Try intriguing variations on familiar themes, like the combination of cranberries and wild rice or chestnuts and potatoes. Serve decorative dishes — a mound of cauliflower and broccoli or a vegetable wreath. Dazzle your family with a traditional Yule Log Cake, prepared easily using microwave shortcuts.

Make-ahead directions for many of the recipes are an important feature of this section. To eliminate last-minute rush and give yourself leisure to enjoy the holiday, do some preparation in advance and finish them just before serving time.

Holiday Events

Festive events, like sleigh rides, caroling and open houses, add to holiday excitement. This section offers ideas for making these occasions as entertaining for you as they are for your guests.

Flexibility makes these suggestions distinctive. A party can look as elaborate as you like, yet be simple to prepare. Make one or two dishes for an intimate group, or expand the menu to serve a crowd. For example, the Dessert Buffet could be a fondue party for eight; using all the dessert recipes provided, a group of friends might cooperate to serve the neighborhood. At a bowl game gathering, pass finger foods to dedicated watchers, provide a substantial buffet for people willing to leave the room, or do both.

A Blizzard of Holiday Ideas

Holiday preparations needn't be all work and no fun. You and your family will enjoy making the treats, gifts and decorations in this section.

To create amusing cookies and candies quickly, use the microwave oven to melt chocolate and candy coating without mess or fuss. Decorations include an edible chocolate candy box which you could fill with candies made in the microwave oven, a glistening nut wreath for the door and dough ornaments for decorating packages and the tree. Indulge your fantasy and build a spectacular village with graham cracker bricks and candy coating mortar.

For gifts, microwave scrumptious dessert sauces or lively condiments. Blend distinctive coffee or tea mixes for the microwavers on your list. As an added help, the gift recipes include suggestions for packaging your gifts artfully.

Holiday Dinner Menus

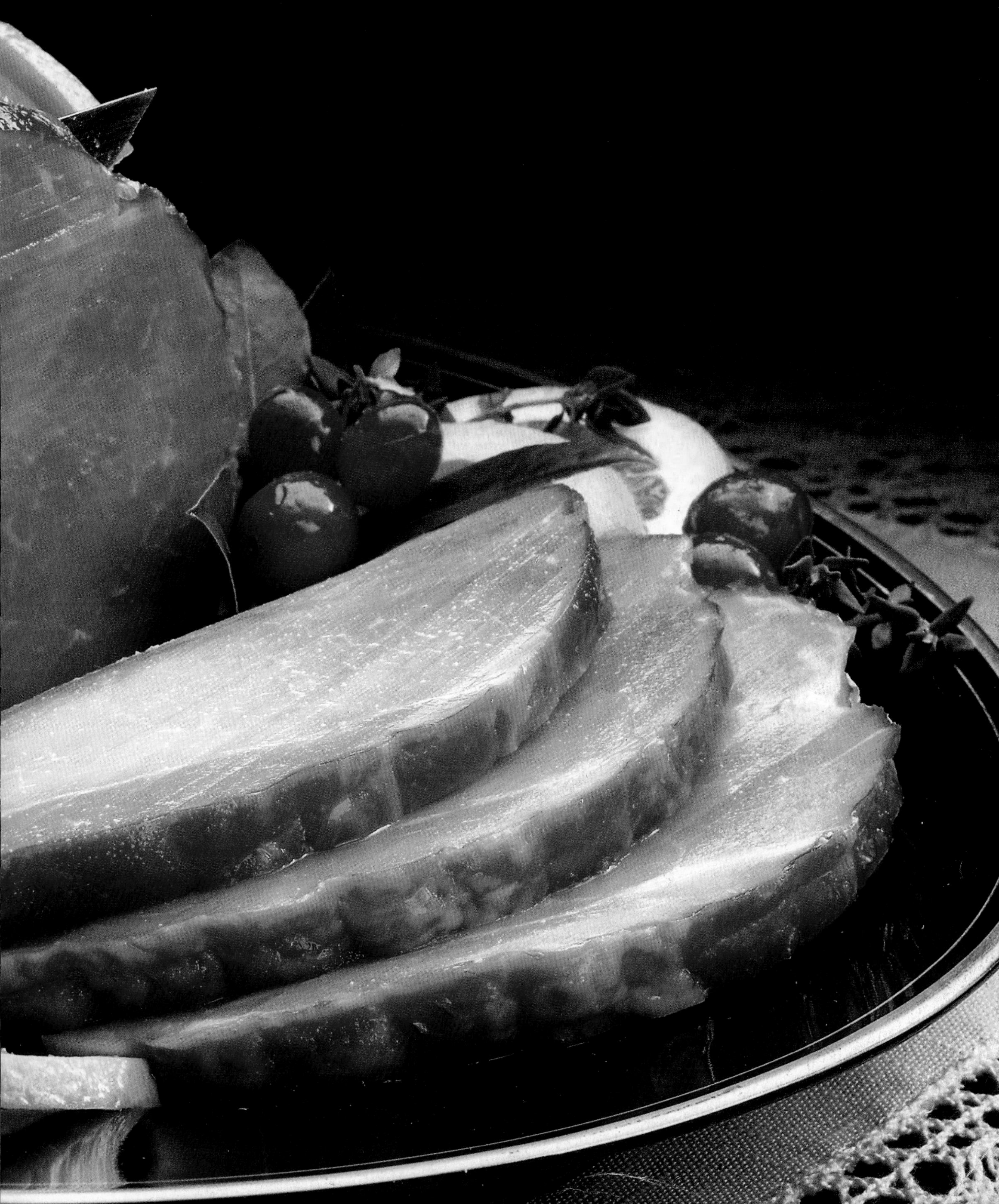

Turkey Dinner

For a large gathering, roast a whole bone-in turkey conventionally and microwave the side dishes. Much of the preparation can be done in advance to reduce last-minute fuss.

To serve a smaller group, microwave a boneless turkey. Although it is possible to microwave a bone-in turkey weighing under 11 pounds, the boneless turkey requires less attention, is easier to carve and has no waste.

Turkey

16 to 20-lb. whole turkey,
    defrosted
    Salt and pepper

2 tablespoons to ¼ cup butter
    or margarine

16 to 20 servings

How to Bake Turkey Conventionally

Heat conventional oven to 325°F. Rinse turkey and pat dry with paper towel. Sprinkle cavity lightly with salt and pepper. Secure legs together with string. Tuck wing tips under. Place turkey in large roasting pan.

Place butter in 1-cup measure. Microwave at High for 45 seconds to 1½ minutes, or until melted. Brush turkey with butter. Sprinkle outside of turkey with salt and pepper. Insert meat thermometer; cover with foil.

Estimate total cooking time at 20 to 30 minutes per pound. Bake until internal temperature in inner thigh registers 185°F. During last 30 minutes, remove foil. Let stand, tented with foil, for 15 to 20 minutes before carving. Reserve drippings for gravy (opposite).

Boneless Herb-roasted Turkey

5 to 6-lb. boneless whole
    turkey
3 cloves garlic, each cut into
    quarters

¾ teaspoon dried marjoram
    leaves
¾ teaspoon dried rosemary
    leaves

¾ teaspoon dried sage leaves
¼ teaspoon pepper

8 to 10 servings

How to Microwave Boneless Herb-roasted Turkey

Cut twelve 1-inch slits in turkey. Insert 1 garlic piece in each slit. In small bowl, combine remaining ingredients. Sprinkle evenly over turkey.

Place turkey in nylon cooking bag. Secure bag loosely with nylon tie or string. Place bag in 10-inch square casserole. Microwave at High for 10 minutes.

Microwave at 70% (Medium High) for 45 minutes to 1¼ hours longer, or until internal temperature registers 185°F in several places, turning turkey over every 30 minutes. Let stand in bag for 15 to 20 minutes before carving. Reserve drippings for gravy (opposite).

Turkey Gravy

2 cups reserved drippings
¼ cup all-purpose flour

¼ teaspoon salt
⅛ teaspoon pepper

2 cups

How to Microwave Turkey Gravy

Strain drippings into 4-cup measure. Add water or chicken broth, if necessary, to equal 2 cups.

Place remaining ingredients in small mixing bowl. Add small amount of drippings to flour mixture. Stir until mixture is smooth. Add back to remaining drippings, stirring with whisk until smooth.

Microwave at High for 6 to 8 minutes, or until mixture thickens and bubbles, stirring 2 or 3 times.

Goose Dinner

Roast the traditional Christmas goose conventionally.
If cooked in a microwave oven, a goose requires a lot of attention
because of its size and high fat content.

While the goose roasts in your conventional oven, microwave the
Crunchy-topped Twice-baked Potatoes. Whole Wheat Fruit Dressing
complements the rich taste of goose, and Cabbage-Apple Sauté
garnishes the platter.

Roast Goose
page 13

Whole Wheat Fruit Dressing
page 44

Cabbage-Apple Sauté
page 35

Marinated Green Bean Salad
page 46

Rolls, Butter, Relishes

Crunchy-topped Twice-baked Potatoes
page 37

Easy Yule Log Cake
page 62

Roast Goose

6 to 8-lb. whole goose

Salt and pepper

6 to 8 servings

How to Roast Goose Conventionally

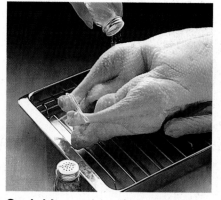

Heat conventional oven to 325°F. Rinse goose and pat dry with paper towel. Sprinkle cavity lightly with salt and pepper. Secure legs together with string. Tuck wing tips under. Place breast-side-up on rack in large roasting pan.

Sprinkle outside of goose with salt and pepper. Estimate total cooking time at 20 to 25 minutes per pound. Roast until legs move freely and juices run clear, basting frequently with drippings. Drain and discard excess fat during roasting.

Cornish Hen Dinner

The festive Cornish game hen is ideal for small holiday dinners serving two to four people. Microwave or bake hens conventionally. Serve them on a bed of Cranberry Wild Rice for a distinctive presentation of the traditional holiday accompaniments.

How to Microwave Red Currant Glaze

Red Currant-glazed Cornish Game Hens

¼ cup red currant jelly
1 tablespoon dry sherry
   Dash ground cinnamon
2 Cornish game hens
   (18 oz. each)
¼ teaspoon salt
⅛ teaspoon pepper

2 servings

Cornish Game Hens for Four:
Follow recipe above, except double all ingredients. Bake conventionally (opposite), or microwave as directed (opposite), except microwave at High for 22 to 32 minutes, rearranging hens twice.

Combine jelly, sherry and cinnamon in 1-cup measure. Mix well.

Microwave at High for 45 seconds to 1½ minutes, or until jelly melts, stirring once. Set aside.

How to Prepare Cornish Game Hens

Remove giblets. Rinse hen cavities with cold water. Pat dry with paper towel.

Sprinkle cavities with salt and pepper. Secure legs together with string.

How to Bake Glazed Cornish Game Hens Conventionally

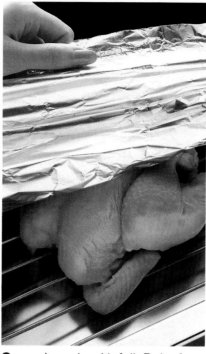

Heat conventional oven to 350°F. Place hens breast-side-up on rack in large roasting pan.

Cover loosely with foil. Bake for 1 hour. Prepare glaze (opposite).

Brush hens with glaze. Roast, uncovered, for 30 minutes, or until golden brown.

How to Microwave Glazed Cornish Game Hens

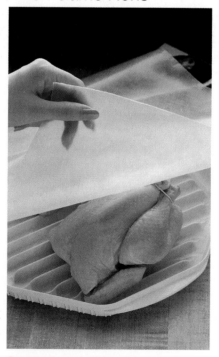

Arrange hens breast-side-up on roasting rack. Set aside. Prepare glaze (opposite). Brush hens with one-half of the glaze.

Cover hens with wax paper. Microwave at High for 12 to 17 minutes, or until legs move freely and juices run clear, rearranging hens once and brushing with remaining glaze once.

Let hens stand, tented with foil, for 5 minutes.

Glazed Ham Dinner

Use the microwave oven to prepare ham for eight to ten people.
When microwaved, a small boneless ham will be juicy. It is easier to roast a large ham
conventionally when serving more than ten people.

Tangy Mustard-glazed Ham
page 19

Festive Melon Ball Mold
page 49

Candied Sweet Potatoes
page 39

Holiday Potato Scallop
page 36

Rolls, Butter, Relishes

Mincemeat Parfaits
page 57

Tangy Mustard-glazed Ham

Conventionally Roasted:

- 1 cup packed brown sugar
- ¼ cup dry mustard
- ¼ cup apple or orange juice
- 8 to 10-lb. fully cooked boneless whole ham
  Whole cloves

16 to 20 servings

Microwaved:

- ½ cup packed brown sugar
- 2 tablespoons dry mustard
- 2 tablespoons apple or orange juice
- 4 to 5-lb. fully cooked boneless whole ham
  Whole cloves

8 to 10 servings

In small mixing bowl, combine all ingredients, except ham and cloves. Mix well. Set aside. Score and spice ham (right). Follow instructions for appropriate cooking method.

How to Score & Spice Ham

Score top of ham in 1-inch diamond pattern, cutting ¼ inch deep. Insert 1 clove in center of each diamond.

How to Roast Glazed Ham Conventionally

Prepare glaze (above). Set aside. Heat conventional oven to 325°F. Insert meat thermometer. Estimate total cooking time at 10 to 15 minutes per pound. Place ham scored-side-up on rack in large roasting pan.

Brush with glaze during last 30 minutes of roasting time. Roast for remaining time, or until internal temperature registers 140°F, basting with drippings once.

Decorate ham with quartered orange slices during last 10 minutes, if desired. Secure orange pieces with cloves in diagonal lines. Baste ham with drippings and return to oven. Let stand for 10 minutes.

How to Microwave Glazed Ham

Place ham scored-side-up in 10-inch square casserole. Cover cut surface with plastic wrap. Insert microwave meat thermometer. Microwave at 50% (Medium) for 30 minutes.

Prepare glaze (above). Brush ham with glaze. Microwave at 50% (Medium) for 10 to 15 minutes, or until internal temperature registers 130°F.

Decorate ham with quartered orange slices (above) during last 5 minutes, if desired. Let stand, tented with foil, for 10 minutes before carving. (Internal temperature will rise 5° to 10°F during standing time.)

19

Pork Crown Roast Dinner

Because it requires a lot of attention, a pork crown roast is more suitable for conventional cooking. Roast it conventionally, then fill with a microwaved dressing. Serve with Broccoli & Cauliflower Ball decorated with lemon slices.

Pork Crown Roast

1½ teaspoons fennel seed, crushed	1 teaspoon pepper
1½ teaspoons onion powder	8-lb. pork crown roast (about 16 ribs)
1 teaspoon salt	Vegetable oil

8 to 10 servings

How to Roast Pork Crown Roast Conventionally

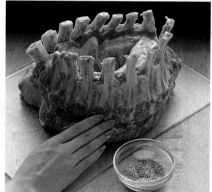 

Combine all ingredients, except roast and oil, in small bowl. Rub mixture on all sides of roast. Cover and refrigerate overnight. Heat conventional oven to 325°F. Place roast on rack in roasting pan. Cover exposed bone ends with foil.

Brush roast lightly with oil. Insert meat thermometer. Estimate total cooking time at 20 minutes per pound. Roast until internal temperature registers 165°F. Let stand for 10 minutes before carving.

Pork Loin Roast Dinner

A boneless pork loin roast can be either cooked conventionally or microwaved.
Microwave Hoppin' John, a Southern favorite, up to two days in advance.
Garnish serving platter with Apples with Coriander & Orange.

Lightly Seasoned Pork Loin Roast with Cream Gravy
page 23   page 23

Lemony Freezer Slaw   *Apples with Coriander & Orange*   *Hoppin' John*
page 47   page 43   page 32

Rolls, Butter, Relishes   *Tipsy Cake*
page 55

Lightly Seasoned Pork Loin Roast

1 teaspoon seasoned salt
¼ teaspoon paprika

3 to 5-lb. boneless pork loin
   roast

6 to 10 servings

How to Roast Pork Loin Roast Conventionally

Heat conventional oven to 325°F. In small bowl, combine salt and paprika. Rub mixture on all sides of roast. Place roast fattiest-side-up on rack in large roasting pan.

Insert meat thermometer. Estimate total cooking time at 30 to 35 minutes per pound. Roast until internal temperature registers 165°F.

Let roast stand for 10 minutes before carving. Strain and reserve drippings for gravy (below).

How to Microwave Pork Loin Roast

Combine salt and paprika in small bowl. Rub mixture on all sides of roast. Place roast fattiest-side-down on roasting rack. Estimate total cooking time at 20 minutes per pound.

Divide time in half. Microwave at 50% (Medium) for first half of total cooking time. Turn roast fattiest-side-up. Insert microwave meat thermometer in roast.

Microwave at 50% (Medium) for second half of cooking time, or until internal temperature registers 160°F in several places. Let stand, tented with foil, for 10 minutes. Strain and reserve drippings for gravy (below).

Cream Gravy

⅔ cup reserved drippings
⅓ cup half-and-half or milk
2 tablespoons all-purpose flour
⅛ teaspoon salt
   Dash pepper

1 cup

Strain drippings into 2-cup measure. Add water, if necessary, to equal ⅔ cup. Add half-and-half. Place remaining ingredients in small mixing bowl. Add small amount of drippings to flour mixture. Stir until mixture is smooth. Add back to remaining drippings, stirring with whisk until smooth. Microwave at High for 3 to 5 minutes, or until mixture thickens and bubbles, stirring twice.

Rib Roast Dinner

Depending on your timetable or your preference, you may microwave the rolled rib roast or roast it conventionally. The Yorkshire Pudding, which requires conventional baking to develop a crust, can be baked while you microwave the meat, or while a conventionally prepared roast stands.

Peppered Rib Roast
page 25

Date & Cherry Molds
page 48

Holiday Yorkshire Pudding
pages 40-41

Brussels Sprouts with Two Mustards
page 32

Rolls, Butter, Relishes

Strawberry-Amaretto Trifle
page 55

Peppered Rib Roast

2 teaspoons coarsely ground pepper
¾ teaspoon garlic powder
½ teaspoon salt (optional)
4 to 6-lb. boneless beef rolled rib roast

8 to 12 servings

Conventional Doneness	Internal Temperature
Very rare	120°F
Medium rare	125°F
Medium	135°F
Well	150°F

How to Roast Peppered Rib Roast Conventionally

Heat conventional oven to 325°F. In small bowl, combine all ingredients, except roast. Rub mixture on all sides of roast.

Place roast fattiest-side-up on rack in large roasting pan; insert meat thermometer. Estimate total cooking time at 25 to 35 minutes per pound.

Roast until internal temperature registers desired doneness (chart above). Let roast stand for 15 to 20 minutes before carving.

How to Microwave Peppered Rib Roast

Combine all ingredients, except roast, in small bowl. Rub mixture on all sides of roast. Place roast fattiest-side-down on roasting rack. Estimate total cooking time at 12 to 15 minutes per pound. Divide cooking time in half.

Microwave at High for 5 minutes. Microwave at 50% (Medium) for remaining part of first half of total cooking time. Turn roast fattiest-side-up. Insert microwave meat thermometer.

Microwave at 50% (Medium) for second half of cooking time, or until internal temperature registers 125°F. Let stand, tented with foil, for 10 minutes before carving. (Internal temperature will rise 5° to 10°F during standing time.)

How to Lace Rack of Lamb

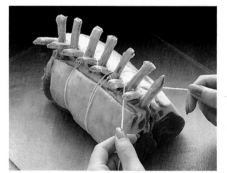

Stand racks on backbone edges, with concave sides facing. Press together, interlacing bone ends. Tie racks together with string, weaving around crossed ribs.

Rack of Lamb Dinner

For an elegant dinner for two, divide a single rack of lamb, lace it together and microwave. Gingered Acorn Squash can be microwaved in advance and reheated while the roast stands. To serve four, make your roast from two racks and bake it conventionally.

Wine-marinated Rack of Lamb

Conventionally Baked:
2 single racks of lamb (1¼ lbs.,
   about 7 to 8 ribs each), rib
   ends exposed
1 cup rosé wine
2 cloves garlic, minced
1 teaspoon dried rosemary
   leaves

4 servings

Microwaved:
1 single rack of lamb
   (1¼ lbs., about 7 to 8 ribs),
   rib ends exposed, cut in half
½ cup rosé wine
1 clove garlic, minced
½ teaspoon dried rosemary
   leaves

2 servings

Place tied racks of lamb (opposite) in nylon cooking bag. Add remaining ingredients. Secure bag with nylon tie or string. Refrigerate overnight, turning bag several times.

How to Roast Rack of Lamb Conventionally

Heat conventional oven to 325°F. Place lamb on rack in large roasting pan. Insert meat thermometer. Estimate total cooking time at 20 minutes per pound.

Roast until internal temperature registers desired doneness (chart below).

Let lamb stand for 10 minutes before carving.

How to Microwave Rack of Lamb

Place lamb on roasting rack. Insert microwave meat thermometer. Microwave at 50% (Medium) for 11 to 20 minutes, or until internal temperature registers desired doneness (chart right), rotating lamb ¼ turn 2 or 3 times.

Let stand, tented with foil, for 10 minutes before carving. (Internal temperature will rise 5° to 10°F during standing time.) Not recommended for ovens with less than 600 cooking watts.

Conventional Doneness	Internal Temperature
Rare	130°F
Medium	145°F
Well	160°F

Microwave Doneness	Internal Temperature
Rare	120°F
Medium	135°F
Well	150°F

Vegetables

Creamy Dilled Vegetable Medley

1 tablespoon butter or
   margarine
1 tablespoon all-purpose flour
½ teaspoon instant chicken
   bouillon granules
⅛ teaspoon dried dill weed
½ cup milk
¼ cup sour cream
2 cups julienne carrots
   (1½ × ¼-inch strips)
1 medium zucchini, cut in half
   lengthwise and thinly sliced
2 tablespoons water

6 to 8 servings

In 2-cup measure, microwave butter at High for 45 seconds to 1 minute, or until melted. Stir in flour, bouillon and dill weed. Blend in milk. Microwave at High for 2 to 2½ minutes, or until mixture thickens and bubbles, stirring after every minute. Add sour cream. Mix well.✳ Set aside.

In 2-quart casserole, combine remaining ingredients. Cover. Microwave at High for 8 to 10 minutes, or until vegetables are tender, stirring once. Drain. Add sauce. Toss to coat. Re-cover. Microwave at High for 2 to 3 minutes, or until hot, stirring once.

Advance preparation: Up to 2 days in advance, cut vegetables. Sprinkle with 1 to 2 teaspoons cold water and store in covered container. Prepare recipe to ✳ above. Cover with plastic wrap and refrigerate. To serve, continue as directed.

Gingered Acorn Squash

¼ cup flaked coconut
2 acorn squash (1½ lbs. each)
¼ cup butter or margarine,
　　cut up
2 tablespoons maple syrup
1 teaspoon finely chopped
　　fresh gingerroot

8 servings

Advance preparation: Up to 3 days in advance, toast coconut. Store in airtight container. Up to 1 day in advance, prepare squash halves to ✳ below. Refrigerate after standing time. To serve, quarter squash and continue as directed, except after pouring butter mixture over squash, microwave at High for 8 to 13 minutes, or until hot.

Sprinkle coconut in 9-inch pie plate. Microwave at High for 3 to 4 minutes, or until lightly browned, tossing with fork after the first minute and then every 30 seconds. Set aside.

Pierce each squash twice with fork and place in microwave oven. Microwave at High for 3 to 4 minutes, or until warm. (This makes it easier to cut squash.) Cut in half lengthwise. Remove seeds from each half.

Wrap each half in plastic wrap and arrange cut-side-up in microwave oven. Microwave at High for 8 to 12 minutes, or until tender, rotating and rearranging once. Let stand, covered, for 5 minutes. ✳

Remove plastic wrap and cut each half lengthwise into quarters. Arrange quarters cut-side-up on 12-inch platter or in 10-inch square casserole. Set aside.

Combine remaining ingredients in 2-cup measure. Microwave at High for 1¼ to 1½ minutes, or until butter melts. Stir to combine. Pour butter mixture over squash. Microwave at High for 4 to 6 minutes, or until hot. Sprinkle with toasted coconut.

31

Brussels Sprouts with Two Mustards ▲

1 tablespoon butter or margarine
1 tablespoon Dijon mustard
2 teaspoons stone-ground mustard

2 teaspoons honey
¼ teaspoon salt
2 pkgs. (10 oz. each) frozen Brussels sprouts

8 servings

In 1½-quart casserole, microwave butter at High for 45 seconds to 1 minute, or until melted. Stir in mustards, honey and salt. Add Brussels sprouts and toss to coat. Cover. Microwave at High for 10 to 14 minutes, or until Brussels sprouts are tender-crisp, stirring once or twice.

Hoppin' John

4 slices bacon, cut into 1-inch pieces
½ cup chopped green pepper
¼ cup sliced green onions
1½ cups uncooked instant rice
1 pkg. (10 oz.) frozen black-eyed peas

1½ cups hot water
½ teaspoon salt
¼ teaspoon dried thyme leaves
⅛ teaspoon pepper
Dash cayenne

8 servings

Place bacon in 2-quart casserole. Cover. Microwave at High for 4 to 5 minutes, or until brown and crisp. Do not drain. Add green pepper and onions. Re-cover. Microwave at High for 1½ to 3 minutes, or until vegetables are tender-crisp.

Stir in remaining ingredients. Re-cover. Microwave at High for 10 to 13 minutes, or until rice and peas are tender and water is absorbed.

Advance preparation: Up to 2 days in advance, prepare as directed above and refrigerate. To serve, cover and microwave at High for 4 to 7 minutes, or until hot, stirring once.

Honeyed Sweet Potatoes & Peas

3 cups peeled, cubed sweet potatoes (½-inch cubes), about 1½ lbs.
2 tablespoons butter or margarine
1 tablespoon honey
½ teaspoon dry mustard
¼ teaspoon salt
1 cup frozen peas

6 to 8 servings

In 1½-quart casserole, combine all ingredients, except peas. Cover. Microwave at High for 8 to 9 minutes, or until sweet potatoes are tender, stirring once. Add peas. Re-cover. Microwave at High for 3 to 5 minutes, or until hot, stirring once.

Crispy Toast Cups ▶

8   slices soft white bread, crusts
      trimmed
2   tablespoons butter or
      margarine

8 servings

Heat conventional oven to 350°F.
Carefully press each bread slice
into ungreased muffin cup. In 1-
cup measure, microwave butter
at High for 45 seconds to 1 minute, or until melted. Brush bread
with butter. Bake for 20 to 25 minutes, or until light golden brown.
Fill with creamed vegetables.

Advance preparation: Up to
2 days in advance, prepare as
directed above. Store in airtight container.

Creamy Tarragon Peas & Onions ▲

1   tablespoon butter or
      margarine
1½ cups pearl onions, peeled
1½ cups frozen peas

Sauce:
2   tablespoons butter or
      margarine

1   tablespoon plus 1 teaspoon
      all-purpose flour
¼   teaspoon salt
¼   teaspoon grated lemon peel
⅛   teaspoon dried tarragon
      leaves
      Dash white pepper
1   cup half-and-half

8 servings

Advance preparation: Up to 2
days in advance, prepare onions
and peas to ✳ below. Cover and
refrigerate. To serve, continue as
directed.

How to Microwave Creamy Tarragon Peas & Onions

Place 1 tablespoon butter in 1½-
quart casserole. Microwave at
High for 45 seconds to 1 minute,
or until melted. Add onions. Cover.
Microwave at High for 3 to 5 minutes, or until tender, stirring once.
Stir in peas. ✳ Set aside.

Place 2 tablespoons butter in
4-cup measure. Microwave at
High for 45 seconds to 1 minute,
or until melted. Stir in remaining
sauce ingredients, except half-
and-half. Blend in half-and-half.
Microwave at High for 3 to 4 minutes, or until mixture thickens and
bubbles, stirring twice.

Pour sauce over peas and
onions. Stir to blend. Microwave
at High for 1 to 2 minutes, or until
hot. Spoon evenly into Crispy
Toast Cups (above), if desired.

33

Broccoli & Cauliflower Ball ▶

4 cups fresh broccoli flowerets
4 cups fresh cauliflowerets
2 tablespoons water
6 thin strips red pepper
3 tablespoons butter or
   margarine
2 teaspoons lemon juice
¼ teaspoon onion salt
   Zest of one lemon
   Lemon slices

6 to 8 servings

Advance preparation: Up to 1 day in advance, prepare to ✳ below. Refrigerate. To serve, continue as directed.

How to Microwave Broccoli & Cauliflower Ball

Combine broccoli, cauliflower and water in 2-quart casserole. Cover. Microwave at High for 5 to 9 minutes, or until vegetables are very hot and color brightens, stirring once. Rinse with cold water. Drain.

Arrange red pepper in 1½-quart deep mixing bowl. Arrange broccoli and cauliflower over red pepper, pressing floweret ends toward outside of bowl. (Alternate rows of broccoli and cauliflower, if desired.) Set aside.

Place butter, lemon juice and onion salt in 1-cup measure. Microwave at High for 1 to 1¼ minutes, or until butter melts. Pour evenly over broccoli and cauliflower. Cover with plastic wrap. ✳

Microwave vegetables at High for 4 to 11 minutes, or until hot, rotating bowl once. Remove plastic wrap. Place serving plate over top of bowl and invert. Sprinkle with lemon zest, and garnish with lemon slices.

Cabbage-Apple Sauté ▲

- 4 slices bacon, cut into 1-inch pieces
- 2 tablespoons sugar
- 2 tablespoons white vinegar
- ½ teaspoon salt
- ½ teaspoon dried marjoram leaves
- 6 cups shredded red cabbage
- 2 cups sliced Granny Smith apples (about ⅛-inch slices)
- ⅓ cup hazelnuts

8 servings

Place bacon in 2-quart casserole. Cover. Microwave at High for 4 to 6 minutes, or until brown and crisp. Do not drain. Stir in sugar, vinegar, salt and marjoram. Microwave at High for 1 minute.

Stir in cabbage and apples. Cover. Microwave at High for 5 to 6 minutes, or until cabbage and apples are tender-crisp, stirring once. Stir in hazelnuts.

Cranberry Wild Rice

- 2 cups water
- 1 cup uncooked wild rice
- 1 cup whole-berry cranberry sauce
- 3 tablespoons dry sherry
- ¼ teaspoon salt
- ½ cup chopped walnuts

6 to 8 servings

In 2-quart saucepan, combine all ingredients, except walnuts. Bring to a boil conventionally over high heat. Reduce heat to low. Cover. Simmer for 35 to 45 minutes, or until rice kernels are open and almost all water is absorbed. Let stand, covered, for 15 minutes. ✳ Stir in walnuts.

Advance preparation: Up to 2 days in advance, cook rice mixture to ✳ above. Cover and refrigerate. To serve, place in 1-quart casserole. Stir in walnuts. Cover. Microwave at High for 6 to 7 minutes, or until hot, stirring once.

Holiday Potato Scallop ▲

6 cups peeled, sliced potatoes
  (⅛-inch slices)
¼ cup sliced green onions
3 tablespoons all-purpose flour
½ teaspoon salt

¼ teaspoon dried thyme leaves
⅛ teaspoon white pepper
2 cups half-and-half
⅓ cup snipped fresh parsley
  Sliced pimiento

6 to 8 servings

In 3-quart casserole, combine all ingredients, except half-and-half, parsley and pimiento. Pour half-and-half over potato mixture. Toss gently to coat. Cover. Microwave at High for 6 minutes. Microwave at 50% (Medium) for 25 to 40 minutes longer, or until potatoes are tender and sauce is thickened, stirring twice.

Spoon potatoes into serving dish. Sprinkle parsley in wreath shape over potatoes. Arrange pimiento to form bow on wreath.

Holiday Au Gratin Potatoes: Follow recipe above, except stir in 1 cup shredded Swiss cheese at end of cooking time. Cover. Let stand for 1 to 2 minutes, or until cheese melts.

Mashed Potatoes

2 lbs. potatoes, peeled and
  quartered
¼ cup water
¼ to ⅓ cup milk
¼ cup butter or margarine
½ teaspoon salt
⅛ teaspoon pepper

6 to 8 servings

In 2-quart casserole, combine potatoes and water. Cover. Microwave at High for 12 to 18 minutes, or until tender, stirring once. Let potatoes stand, covered, for 5 minutes. Drain.

In medium mixing bowl, place potatoes and remaining ingredients. Mash with a potato masher, or beat at medium speed of electric mixer, until mixture is smooth.

36

Baked Potatoes & Baked Sweet Potatoes

Potatoes	Time (High)
2 (8-10 oz. each)	5-10 min.
4 (8-10 oz. each)	10-16 min.
6 (8-10 oz. each)	18-25 min.

Sweet Potatoes	Time (High)
2 (8-10 oz. each)	8-10 min.
4 (8-10 oz. each)	12-18 min.
6 (8-10 oz. each)	20-30 min.

Pierce potatoes with fork. Place on roasting rack or paper towel and arrange in a circle in micro-wave oven. Microwave at High as directed in chart above, or just until tender, turning over and rearranging once. Let stand for 5 minutes.

Advance preparation: Up to 45 minutes in advance, microwave potatoes. Wrap each in foil to keep hot.

Crunchy-topped Twice-baked Potatoes ▲

- 4 medium baking potatoes (8 to 10 oz. each)
- 2 tablespoons butter or margarine
- ¼ cup half-and-half
- 1 egg
- 1 tablespoon chopped pimiento
- ¼ teaspoon salt
- ⅛ teaspoon cayenne
- 1 pkg. (3 oz.) cream cheese

Topping:
- ½ cup seasoned dry bread crumbs
- ⅓ cup chopped pecans
- 1 teaspoon dried parsley flakes
- 3 tablespoons butter or margarine

8 servings

Pierce potatoes with fork. Arrange in a circle on paper towel in micro-wave oven. Microwave at High for 10 to 16 minutes, or just until tender, turning over and rearranging once. Let cool slightly. Cut potatoes in half lengthwise. Scoop out and reserve pulp, leaving ¼-inch shells. Set shells aside.

In medium mixing bowl, combine pulp and remaining ingredients, except cream cheese and topping. In small bowl, microwave cream cheese at High for 15 to 30 seconds, or until softened. Add to potato mixture. Beat at medium speed of electric mixer until smooth. Pipe or spoon mixture evenly into shells.✷ Set aside.

In small mixing bowl, combine bread crumbs, pecans and parsley. In small bowl, microwave 3 tablespoons butter at High for 1 to 1¼ minutes, or until melted. Add to bread crumb mixture. Toss to coat. Top each potato with about 1 tablespoon mixture, pressing so crumbs adhere. Arrange potatoes in 10-inch square casserole. Microwave at High for 9 to 11 minutes, or until hot, rotating dish and rearranging pota-toes once.

Advance preparation: Up to 1 month in advance, prepare potatoes to ✷ above. Wrap in foil and freeze. To serve, continue as directed, except cover and microwave potatoes at High for 10 minutes, rotating dish once. Top with bread crumb mixture. Microwave at High, un-covered, for 5 to 7 minutes, or until hot.

Creamy Stuffed Sweet Potatoes ▲

3 sweet potatoes (12 to
   16 oz. each)
2 tablespoons butter or
   margarine

¾ cup half-and-half
¼ cup orange marmalade
¼ teaspoon salt
2 tablespoons sliced almonds

6 servings

Pierce sweet potatoes with fork. Arrange in circle on paper towel in microwave oven. Microwave at High for 10 to 13 minutes, or just until tender, turning over and rearranging once. Let cool slightly. Cut potatoes in half lengthwise. Scoop out and reserve pulp, leaving about ¼-inch shells. Set shells aside.

In medium mixing bowl, combine pulp and remaining ingredients, except almonds. Beat at medium speed of electric mixer until smooth. Pipe or spoon mixture evenly into shells. ✳ Sprinkle each potato with 1 teaspoon almonds. Arrange potatoes in 10-inch square casserole. Cover. Microwave at High for 10 to 12 minutes, or until hot, rotating dish and rearranging potatoes once.

Advance preparation: Up to 1 month in advance, prepare potatoes to ✳ above. Wrap in foil and freeze. To serve, continue as directed, except microwave at High for 10 minutes. Sprinkle with almonds. Microwave at High for 5 to 7 minutes, or until hot, rotating dish and rearranging potatoes once.

Sherried Sweet Potatoes

2 cans (18 oz. each) sweet
   potatoes, drained
½ cup apricot nectar
2 eggs
2 tablespoons honey
2 tablespoons dry sherry
½ teaspoon salt
¼ teaspoon ground nutmeg
¼ cup chopped pecans

6 to 8 servings

In large mixing bowl, combine all ingredients, except pecans. Beat at medium speed of electric mixer until light and fluffy. Spread mixture in 10-inch pie plate. ✳ Sprinkle evenly with pecans. Cover with wax paper. Microwave at High for 4 minutes. Microwave at 50% (Medium) for 9 to 15 minutes longer, or until center is set, rotating dish once or twice.

Advance preparation: Up to 2 days in advance, prepare sweet potato mixture to ✳ above. Cover with plastic wrap and refrigerate. To serve, continue as directed, except microwave at 50% (Medium) for 12 to 20 minutes, or until center is set, rotating dish once or twice.

Dijon Potatoes & Chestnuts ▶

1½ cups fresh chestnuts (about 7 oz.)
1 cup water
¼ cup butter or margarine
2 tablespoons Dijon mustard
½ teaspoon sugar
⅛ teaspoon dried dill weed
4 cups quartered new potatoes (about 2 lbs.)
½ cup julienne red pepper (1½ × ¼-inch strips)
½ cup snipped fresh parsley

8 servings

Make a horizontal cut through rounded part of shell of each chestnut without cutting into nutmeat. Place chestnuts and water in 1½-quart casserole. Cover. Microwave at High for 3 to 4 minutes, or until water boils. Microwave at High for 1 minute longer. Let stand for 10 minutes. Rinse with cold water. Peel shell and inner skin from each chestnut. Cut each chestnut in half.✳ Set aside.

Place butter in 2-quart casserole. Microwave at High for 1¼ to 1½ minutes, or until melted. Stir in mustard, sugar and dill weed. Add chestnuts, potatoes and red pepper. Toss to coat. Cover. Microwave at High for 15 to 20 minutes, or until potatoes are tender, stirring twice. Stir in parsley.

Advance preparation: Up to 1 day in advance, prepare chestnuts to ✳ above. Place in covered container and refrigerate. To serve, continue as directed.

Candied Sweet Potatoes

2 sweet potatoes (12 to 16 oz. each), peeled and sliced (about 4 cups)
2 tablespoons butter or margarine
½ cup packed brown sugar
2 tablespoons light corn syrup
1 tablespoon unsweetened pineapple juice
⅛ teaspoon ground allspice
2 cups miniature marshmallows

6 to 8 servings

Arrange sweet potato slices, slightly overlapping, in 10-inch pie plate. Set aside. In 1-cup measure, microwave butter at High for 45 seconds to 1 minute, or until melted. Stir in remaining ingredients, except marshmallows. Pour evenly over potatoes. Cover with plastic wrap. Microwave at High for 8 to 11 minutes, or until tender, rotating dish once. Remove plastic wrap. Sprinkle potatoes with marshmallows. Place under conventional broiler, 8 inches from heat. Broil just until marshmallows are light golden brown, about 1 minute.

Holiday Yorkshire Pudding

1¾ cups all-purpose flour
 1 teaspoon seasoned salt
 1 cup milk
 4 eggs
 1 cup cold water
 2 cups fresh broccoli flowerets
 2 tablespoons water
⅓ cup reserved beef
    drippings or butter
½ cup thin strips carrot or
    carrot curls

8 to 10 servings

Advance preparation: Up to 1½ hours in advance, prepare batter to ✳ below. If serving pudding with Peppered Rib Roast (page 25), bake while roast is standing.

How to Make Holiday Yorkshire Pudding

Combine flour and salt in medium mixing bowl. Make a well in flour. Pour milk into well and stir to combine. In medium mixing bowl, beat eggs at medium speed of electric mixer until light and fluffy.

Add eggs to flour and milk mixture and continue to beat just until smooth. Add water and beat just until large bubbles rise to the surface, about 30 seconds. Cover with plastic wrap and refrigerate batter for 1 hour. ✳

Combine broccoli and 2 tablespoons water in 2-quart casserole. Cover and microwave at High for 2 to 3 minutes, or until broccoli is very hot and color brightens. Rinse with cold water. Drain. Set aside.

40

Heat conventional oven to 400°F. Place beef drippings in bottom of 9 × 13-inch or 3-quart glass baking dish. Place in oven for about 3 minutes, or until drippings are hot and melted.

Remove batter from refrigerator. Beat at medium speed of electric mixer until large bubbles rise to the surface, about 30 seconds.

Pour batter into heated baking dish. Sprinkle with broccoli and carrots. Bake for 20 minutes. Reduce oven temperature to 350°F. Bake for 10 to 20 minutes longer, or until edges are deep golden brown. Serve immediately.

Fruit Garnishes

◄ Fruit Glacé

½ cup dried apricot halves
½ cup dried calimyrna figs
½ cup dried peach halves
¾ cup apple juice, divided
¼ teaspoon ground cardamom
2 teaspoons cornstarch
1 cup seedless green grapes
1 cup seedless red grapes

6 to 8 servings

In 1½-quart casserole, combine apricots, figs and peaches. Add ½ cup apple juice and the cardamom. Cover. Microwave at High for 5 to 8 minutes, or until fruits are plumped, stirring once.

In small bowl, combine cornstarch and remaining ¼ cup apple juice. Stir until smooth. Add to fruit mixture. Mix well. Microwave at High, uncovered, for 1½ to 2½ minutes, or until mixture is thickened and translucent, stirring once. Add grapes. Stir gently to coat. Spoon as garnish around Pork Crown Roast (page 21) or Glazed Ham (page 18), if desired.

Advance preparation: Up to 2 days in advance, prepare as directed above and serve cold, if desired. To reheat, microwave at High, covered, for 1½ to 2½ minutes, or until hot, stirring once.

Apples with Coriander & Orange ▲

2 tablespoons butter or margarine
2 medium Rome apples, cored and cut into ½-inch cubes (about 3 cups)
2 tablespoons packed brown sugar
½ teaspoon grated orange peel
¼ teaspoon ground coriander

6 to 8 servings

In 1-quart casserole, microwave butter at High for 45 seconds to 1 minute. Add remaining ingredients. Toss gently to coat. Cover. Microwave at High for 3 to 4 minutes, or until apples are tender, stirring once. Spoon as garnish around Lightly Seasoned Pork Loin Roast (page 23), if desired.

Dressings

Whole Wheat Fruit Dressing

½ cup butter or margarine
¼ cup sliced green onions
6 cups soft whole wheat bread cubes
1 cup chopped dried fruit
½ cup chopped pecans
½ teaspoon grated orange peel
1 medium orange, peeled and chopped (about ½ cup)
½ teaspoon salt
¼ teaspoon ground allspice
1 cup water

8 servings

In large mixing bowl, microwave butter at High for 1½ to 1¾ minutes, or until melted. Add onions. Microwave at High for 1 minute. Stir in remaining ingredients. Spoon into 9-inch square baking dish.✳ Cover with wax paper. Microwave at High for 5 to 7 minutes, or until hot, stirring once.

Advance preparation: Up to 2 days in advance, prepare as directed to ✳ above. Cover with plastic wrap and refrigerate. To serve, cover with wax paper. Microwave at High for 7 to 9 minutes, or until hot, stirring once.

Rice & Sausage Dressing ▲

½ cup butter or margarine
½ cup chopped onion
½ cup chopped green pepper
½ cup chopped carrot
4 cups cooked long-grain white or brown rice
1 pkg. (8 oz.) frozen, fully cooked pork sausage links, cut into ½-inch pieces
½ teaspoon salt
½ teaspoon dried thyme leaves
¼ teaspoon garlic powder
⅛ teaspoon pepper

8 servings

In large mixing bowl, microwave butter at High for 1½ to 1¾ minutes, or until melted. Add onion, green pepper and carrot. Cover with plastic wrap. Microwave at High for 3 to 4 minutes, or until vegetables are tender, stirring once. Stir in remaining ingredients. Spoon into 2-quart casserole. Re-cover.✳ Microwave at High for 7 to 9 minutes, or until hot, stirring once.

Advance preparation: Up to 2 days in advance, prepare as directed to ✳ above. Refrigerate. To serve, microwave at High for 10 to 12 minutes, or until hot, stirring once.

Lemon Sage Dressing ▶

½ cup butter or margarine
1 cup sliced celery
½ cup sliced green onions
½ cup shredded carrot
8 cups unseasoned stuffing cubes
½ teaspoon grated lemon peel
½ teaspoon dried sage leaves
½ teaspoon salt
⅛ teaspoon pepper
1½ cups ready-to-serve chicken broth

8 servings

In large mixing bowl, microwave butter at High for 1½ to 1¾ minutes, or until melted. Add celery, onions and carrot. Cover with plastic wrap. Microwave at High for 3 to 4 minutes, or until vegetables are tender, stirring once. Stir in remaining ingredients. Recover. ✳ Microwave at High for 5 to 8 minutes, or until hot, stirring once or twice.

Advance preparation: Up to 2 days in advance, prepare as directed to ✳ above. Refrigerate. To serve, microwave at High, covered, for 9 to 12 minutes, or until hot, stirring once.

Spicy Couscous Dressing

1 cup ready-to-serve chicken broth
1 cup water
1 cup uncooked couscous
¼ cup chopped red pepper
¼ cup chopped green pepper
1 tablespoon butter or margarine
1 can (5 oz.) corn, drained
2 tablespoons snipped fresh parsley
½ teaspoon salt
¼ to ½ teaspoon cayenne
¼ teaspoon ground cumin

8 servings

In 2-quart casserole, place chicken broth and water. Cover. Microwave at High for 4 to 5 minutes, or until mixture boils. Add couscous. Microwave, uncovered, at High for 2 minutes. Let stand for 15 minutes, covered, or until couscous is tender and liquid is absorbed.

In small mixing bowl, combine peppers and butter. Cover with plastic wrap. Microwave at High for 2 to 3 minutes, or until peppers are tender-crisp. Add peppers and remaining ingredients to couscous. Mix well. Microwave at High for 3 to 5 minutes, or until hot, stirring once.

Advance preparation: Up to 2 days in advance, prepare as directed above. Cover and refrigerate. To serve, microwave at High, covered, for 4 to 6 minutes, or until hot, stirring once.

Salads

Strawberry-Avocado Salad ▲

6 cups trimmed and torn curly
      endive
2 cups fresh strawberries, hulled
      and sliced
1 avocado, sliced

Dressing:
⅓ cup honey
⅓ cup orange juice
⅓ cup vegetable oil
1 tablespoon poppy seed

6 to 8 servings

In large mixing bowl, toss endive, strawberries and avocado. Set aside.

In 2-cup measure, combine dressing ingredients. Microwave at High for 45 seconds to 1 minute, or until hot. Pour over endive mixture and toss to coat. Serve immediately.

Advance preparation: Up to 1 day in advance, combine dressing ingredients and refrigerate. To serve, toss endive, strawberries and avocado in large mixing bowl. Microwave dressing for 1½ to 2 minutes, or until hot. Pour over endive mixture and toss to coat.

Marinated Green Bean Salad

1 lb. fresh green beans, cut into
      1-inch lengths
½ cup sugar
½ cup white vinegar
1 teaspoon celery seed

¼ teaspoon dry mustard
1 cup fresh mushrooms, cut
      into quarters
1 cup cherry tomatoes, cut
      in half

8 servings

Place green beans in 2-quart casserole. In 2-cup measure, combine remaining ingredients, except mushrooms and tomatoes. Pour vinegar mixture over green beans. Toss to coat.

Microwave at High for 6 to 10 minutes, or until green beans are tender-crisp, stirring twice. Stir in mushrooms and tomatoes. Cover and re-frigerate 4 to 6 hours, or overnight. Use slotted spoon to serve.

Endive-Broccoli Salad

4 cups fresh broccoli flowerets
1 cup julienne red pepper
      (1½ × ¼-inch strips)
2 tablespoons water
4 cups trimmed and torn curly
      endive
½ cup olive oil
¼ cup white wine vinegar
½ teaspoon sugar
½ teaspoon salt
¼ teaspoon dried basil leaves
¼ teaspoon garlic powder
      Dash white pepper
½ cup pitted black olives

8 servings

In 2-quart casserole, combine broccoli, red pepper and water. Cover. Microwave at High for 5 to 6 minutes, or until vegetables are very hot and color brightens, stirring once or twice. Rinse with cold water. Drain. In large mixing bowl, combine broccoli mixture and endive.

In 2-cup measure, combine remaining ingredients, except olives. Microwave at High for 2 to 3 minutes, or until mixture boils, beating well with whisk once. Cool 10 minutes. Pour over broccoli mixture. Toss gently. Sprinkle with olives.

Lemony Freezer Slaw ▶

- 3 cups sliced green cabbage
- 3 cups sliced red cabbage
- 1 cup shredded carrot
- 2 teaspoons grated lemon peel
- 1 cup sugar
- 1 cup white vinegar
- 1 teaspoon poppy seed
- ½ teaspoon salt
- ¼ teaspoon onion powder

8 servings

In large mixing bowl, combine cabbages, carrot and lemon peel. Set aside. In 4-cup measure, combine remaining ingredients. Microwave at High for 4 to 5½ minutes, or until boiling. Cool slightly. Pour over cabbage mixture. Stir gently. Transfer to plastic freezer container. Label and freeze no longer than 1 month.

To serve, remove cover. Microwave at High for 2 minutes. Stir to break apart. Microwave at 50% (Medium) for 4 to 5 minutes, or until defrosted, stirring once. Mixture should still be very cold.

Cranberry Waldorf Salad

Dressing:
- 2 eggs
- ⅓ cup sugar
- ¼ cup orange juice
- 2 tablespoons water
- 2 tablespoons grated orange peel

Salad:
- 2 cups fresh or frozen cranberries, chopped
- 2 medium oranges, peeled and chopped (about 1 cup)
- 1 large apple, chopped (about 1 cup)
- 1 cup chopped dates
- ½ cup chopped walnuts
- 2 cups miniature marshmallows

8 servings

In 4-cup measure, beat eggs well with whisk. Add remaining dressing ingredients. Beat with whisk until mixture is smooth. Microwave at 50% (Medium) for 4 to 6 minutes, or until mixture thickens, beating with whisk every 2 minutes. Chill about 2 hours, or until cold.

In large mixing bowl, combine salad ingredients.✳ Spoon dressing over salad. Toss gently to coat.

Advance preparation: Up to 1 day in advance, prepare as directed to ✳ above, except omit marshmallows. Cover and refrigerate dressing and salad in separate containers. To serve, add marshmallows to salad. Spoon dressing over salad. Toss gently to coat.

Date & Cherry Molds

    2 cups hot water
    1 pkg. (6 oz.) cherry gelatin
1½ cups cold water
1½ cups diced Granny Smith
       apples
    1 cup maraschino cherries,
       cut into quarters
  ¾ cup chopped dates
  ¾ cup blanched almonds,
       chopped
    1 pkg. (3 oz.) cream cheese

8 servings

Brush the inside of eight (6 to 8-oz. each) salad molds or custard cups lightly with vegetable oil. Set aside. Place hot water in medium mixing bowl. Cover with plastic wrap. Microwave at High for 2 to 3 minutes, or until boiling. Stir in gelatin until dissolved. Add cold water. Chill 45 minutes to 1 hour, or until gelatin is soft-set.

Stir in remaining ingredients, except cream cheese. Spoon mixture evenly into prepared molds. Chill 2 hours or until set. ✳

Dip each mold into warm water for 30 seconds. Loosen edges and unmold onto serving plates. In small bowl, microwave cream cheese at High for 15 to 30 seconds, or until softened. Pipe or spoon cream cheese evenly onto each salad.

Advance preparation: Up to 1 day in advance, prepare to ✳ above. Up to 4 hours in advance, unmold onto serving plates and decorate with softened cream cheese. Chill until serving time.

Lemon-Vegetable Wreath ▲

    2 envelopes (0.25 oz. each)
       unflavored gelatin
  ½ cup cold water
2½ cups hot water
  ⅓ cup sugar
  ¼ cup fresh lemon juice
    1 pkg. (6 oz.) frozen pea
       pods

    1 medium cucumber, quartered
       lengthwise and thinly sliced
       (about 1¼ cups)
  ½ cup thinly sliced celery
  ½ cup chopped red pepper
  ½ cup fresh parsley sprigs
    1 teaspoon grated lemon peel
       Leaf lettuce

8 servings

Brush the inside of 6-cup ring mold lightly with vegetable oil. Set aside. In medium mixing bowl, sprinkle gelatin over cold water to soften. Set aside. Place hot water in 4-cup measure. Cover with plastic wrap. Microwave at High for 5 to 8 minutes, or until boiling. Add boiling water to gelatin and stir until gelatin is completely dissolved. Stir in sugar and lemon juice. Chill for 1¾ to 2 hours, or until very cold.

Place pea pods in 1-quart casserole. Cover. Microwave at High for 2 to 2½ minutes, or just until defrosted. Rinse with cold water. Drain. Stir pea pods and remaining ingredients, except lettuce, into gelatin mixture. Pour into prepared ring mold. Chill until set, about 2 hours. ✳

Line serving platter with lettuce. Dip mold into warm water for 30 seconds. Loosen edges and unmold onto platter.

Advance preparation: Up to 1 day in advance, prepare to ✳ above. Up to 4 hours in advance, unmold onto serving platter and chill until serving time.

Festive Melon Ball Mold

- 1 cup hot water
- 1 pkg. (3 oz.) lime gelatin
- ¾ cup cold water
- 2 cups cantaloupe balls
- 1 can (8 oz.) pineapple tidbits, drained
- 1 cup seedless red grapes
- ½ cup sliced celery
  Red-tipped leaf lettuce
- 1 pkg. (3 oz.) cream cheese (optional)

8 servings

Brush the inside of 4 or 5-cup mold lightly with vegetable oil. Set aside. Place hot water in 4-cup measure. Cover with plastic wrap. Microwave at High for 2 to 3 minutes, or until boiling. Stir in gelatin until dissolved. Add cold water. Chill 1½ to 1¾ hours, or until gelatin is soft-set.

Add remaining ingredients, except lettuce and cream cheese. Pour into prepared mold. Chill 2 hours, or until set. ✳ Arrange lettuce leaves on serving platter. Dip mold in hot water for 15 to 20 seconds. Loosen edges and unmold onto serving platter. Chill until serving time.

In small mixing bowl, microwave cream cheese at High for 15 to 30 seconds, or until softened. Stir until smooth. Spoon or pipe as desired onto salad.

Advance preparation: Up to 1 day in advance, prepare mold to ✳ above. Up to 4 hours in advance, unmold onto serving platter and decorate with cream cheese. Chill until serving time.

Holiday Desserts

Orange Pumpkin Pie

1 pkg. (15 oz.) refrigerated
  prepared pie crusts
2 teaspoons sugar
1¼ teaspoons ground
  cinnamon, divided
1 tablespoon milk
  Red and green candied
  cherries

1 can (16 oz.) pumpkin
1 can (14 oz.) sweetened
  condensed milk
2 eggs
1 teaspoon grated orange
  peel
¼ teaspoon ground nutmeg

8 servings

Advance preparation: Up to 1 day in advance, prepare pie to ✳ below and refrigerate. To serve, decorate with pastry bow.

How to Make Orange Pumpkin Pie

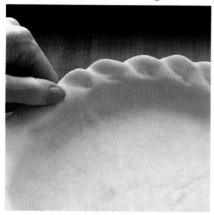

Heat conventional oven to 425°F. Let pie crusts stand at room temperature for 15 to 20 minutes. Unfold 1 crust, ease into 9-inch pie plate and flute edges.

Combine sugar and ¼ teaspoon cinnamon in small bowl. Brush edges of crust lightly with milk. Sprinkle with about ½ teaspoon sugar mixture. Bake for 8 to 10 minutes, or until lightly browned. Cool.

Use remaining crust to form pastry bow and ribbon. Cut 4 strips, each 8 inches by ¾ inch. Place 1 strip on baking sheet. Cross at center with another strip. Secure strips together, using a small amount of cold water.

Form bow over center of crossed strips, squeezing gently in center. Brush bow and ribbon lightly with milk. Sprinkle with remaining sugar mixture. Decorate center with red and green cherries. Bake at 425°F for 6 to 8 minutes, or until lightly browned. Cool.

Combine remaining 1 teaspoon cinnamon and the remaining ingredients in medium mixing bowl. Beat at low speed of electric mixer until mixture is smooth. Microwave at High for 4 to 5 minutes, or until mixture is very hot and starts to set, stirring once or twice.

Pour into prepared pie crust. Place pie plate on saucer in microwave oven. Microwave at 50% (Medium) for 15 to 21 minutes, or until center is set, rotating 3 or 4 times. ✳ Using spatula, carefully loosen bow and ribbon from baking sheet. Place on top of filling. Cool.

Pecan Tarts ▶

1 pkg. (15 oz.) refrigerated
    prepared pie crusts
½ cup chopped pecans
½ cup dark corn syrup
¼ cup packed brown sugar
1 egg
1 tablespoon butter or
    margarine
¼ teaspoon salt
1 tablespoon grated orange
    peel

10 tarts

Advance preparation: Up to
2 days in advance, prepare tart
shells to ✳ below. Cool and store
in airtight containers. Up to 2 hours
in advance, prepare filling and
spoon into tart shells. Cool and
cover loosely with wax paper
until serving time. Sprinkle with
grated orange peel.

How to Make Pecan Tarts

Heat conventional oven to 425°F.
Let pie crusts stand at room temperature for 15 to 20 minutes.
Unfold crusts and place each
crust over five 3½-inch individual
tart pans.

Press top of dough over each
pan lightly with fingers until dough
lines pans. Press rolling pin lightly
over top of pans to cut off excess
dough. Using fork, prick bottom
of crusts several times.

Bake for 10 to 12 minutes, or until
light golden brown. Cool and remove tart shells from pans. Arrange shells on serving platter.✳
Set aside. Combine remaining
ingredients, except orange peel,
in large mixing bowl.

Golden Rum Fruitcake

2 to 3 tablespoons graham
   cracker crumbs
3 eggs
¾ cup packed brown sugar
¾ cup all-purpose flour
½ teaspoon baking powder
¼ teaspoon salt
¼ teaspoon ground allspice

½ teaspoon vanilla
1 cup candied red and green
   cherries
1 cup candied chopped
   pineapple
1 cup walnuts
½ cup golden raisins
   Rum

8 to 12 servings

Generously grease 9-inch ring mold. Sprinkle bottom and sides with graham cracker crumbs. Set aside. In medium mixing bowl, beat eggs and brown sugar until light and fluffy. Beat in flour, baking powder, salt, allspice and vanilla until smooth. Stir in remaining ingredients, except rum. Spoon into prepared ring mold.

Microwave at 50% (Medium) for 10 minutes. Rotate dish one-half turn. Microwave at High for 3 to 6 minutes longer, or until wooden pick inserted in center comes out clean. (Top may still appear moist.) Let stand on counter for 10 minutes.

Invert fruitcake onto plate. Cool 30 minutes. Moisten cheesecloth with rum and wrap fruitcake tightly in cheesecloth. Place in large plastic food-storage bag. Chill at least 24 hours, or up to 2 weeks, before slicing.

Microwave at 50% (Medium) for 8 to 11 minutes, or until mixture thickens and boils slightly, stirring every 2 minutes. Spoon mixture evenly into prepared tart shells. Let cool. (Mixture sets as it cools.) Before serving, sprinkle with grated orange peel.

◄ Strawberry-Amaretto Trifle

- 2 eggs
- ½ cup sugar
- 2 tablespoons quick-cooking tapioca
- 2 cups milk
- ¼ cup plus 1 tablespoon amaretto liqueur, divided
- 2 cups whipping cream
- 1 pint fresh strawberries, hulled and cut in half, reserving 1 whole strawberry for garnish
- 1 un-iced strawberry-filled jelly roll (16-oz.), cut into 1-inch slices

8 servings

In 4-cup measure, beat eggs with whisk until frothy. Beat in sugar, tapioca and milk. Microwave at 50% (Medium) for 15 to 20 minutes, or until mixture thickens and bubbles, beating well twice. Stir in 1 tablespoon liqueur. Place plastic wrap directly on surface of pudding. ✷ Refrigerate 4 to 6 hours, or until very cold. (Mixture thickens as it cools.)

In medium mixing bowl, beat whipping cream until soft peaks form. Reserve ½ cup whipped cream for topping. Fold remaining whipped cream into chilled pudding.

Arrange 1 cup of the strawberries in bottom of 3-quart trifle dish or clear, straight-sided glass bowl. Spoon 1 cup of the pudding mixture over strawberries. Place jelly roll slices upright around inside of bowl, pressing lightly into pudding. Place any remaining jelly roll slices in center. Drizzle remaining ¼ cup liqueur evenly over jelly roll slices. Spoon remaining pudding mixture in center of bowl.

Arrange remaining strawberries around top edge. Spoon reserved ½ cup whipped cream in center. Garnish top with reserved whole strawberry.

Advance preparation: Up to 1 day in advance, prepare pudding to ✷ above and refrigerate. Up to 6 hours in advance, continue recipe as directed, except for garnish. To serve, garnish top with whole strawberry.

Tipsy Cake

- 1 pkg. (3⅛ oz.) vanilla pudding and pie filling
- 2 cups milk
- 1 tablespoon bourbon
- 2 cups whipping cream
- 2 tablespoons powdered sugar
- 1 tablespoon grated orange peel
- 1 pkg. (3 oz.) ladyfingers (about 12 split)
- ½ cup orange marmalade
- ½ cup plus 2 tablespoons raisins, divided
- ½ cup plus 2 tablespoons sliced almonds, divided

8 to 10 servings

Place pudding mix in 4-cup measure. Blend in milk. Microwave at High for 6 to 9 minutes, or until mixture thickens and bubbles, stirring after first 3 minutes and then every minute. Stir in bourbon. Place plastic wrap directly on surface of pudding. Refrigerate until completely cool, about 4 hours or overnight. ✷

Place whipping cream in medium mixing bowl. Beat, gradually adding sugar, until soft peaks form. Fold in orange peel. Set aside.

Spread cut sides of ladyfinger halves with marmalade. Arrange 16 ladyfinger halves marmalade-side-up over bottom and along sides of 3-quart clear glass serving bowl. Sprinkle with ¼ cup raisins and ¼ cup almonds. Spread ½ cup pudding over raisins and almonds. Spread ½ cup whipped cream over pudding. Arrange remaining 8 ladyfingers, marmalade-side-up, on whipped cream. Sprinkle ¼ cup raisins and ¼ cup almonds over ladyfingers. Spread remaining pudding over raisins and almonds. Spread remaining whipped cream over pudding.

Sprinkle top with remaining 2 tablespoons raisins and 2 tablespoons almonds. Garnish with orange slices or thin piece of orange peel, if desired.

Advance preparation: Up to 2 days in advance, prepare recipe as directed to ✷ above. To serve, continue as directed.

Pumpkin Parfait ▲

- 1 cup granulated sugar
- ¼ cup cornstarch
- 2 tablespoons all-purpose flour
- ½ teaspoon ground cinnamon
- ½ teaspoon ground nutmeg
- ½ teaspoon salt
- 1 can (16 oz.) pumpkin
- 2 cups milk
- 1½ cups whipping cream
- 2 tablespoons powdered sugar
- ½ teaspoon vanilla
- 1 cup finely crushed gingersnap cookie crumbs (about 15 gingersnaps)

8 servings

In 3-quart casserole, combine granulated sugar, cornstarch, flour, cinnamon, nutmeg and salt. Add pumpkin and milk. Mix well. Microwave at High for 11 to 18 minutes, or until mixture thickens and bubbles, stirring after the first 3 minutes and then every 2 minutes. Place plastic wrap directly on surface of pudding. ✳ Refrigerate about 4 hours, or until cool.

In small mixing bowl, beat whipping cream, gradually adding powdered sugar, until soft peaks form. Fold in vanilla. In each of eight 8-oz. parfait or wine glasses, layer scant 1 tablespoon cookie crumbs, 2 tablespoons pudding, 2 tablespoons whipped cream, scant 1 tablespoon cookie crumbs, 2 tablespoons pudding. Top each parfait with dollop of whipped cream (about 1 tablespoon) and a sprinkle of cookie crumbs.

Advance preparation: Up to 1 day in advance, prepare pudding to ✳ above and refrigerate. Up to 2 hours in advance, assemble parfaits.

How to Microwave Mincemeat Parfaits

◄ Mincemeat Parfaits

1 pkg. (3⅛ oz.) vanilla
   pudding and pie filling
2 cups milk
2 cups prepared mincemeat
½ teaspoon imitation rum
   extract
2 jars (6 oz. each) maraschino
   cherries, drained
2½ cups prepared whipped
   topping, divided

8 servings

Advance preparation: Up to 1 day in advance, prepare pudding, mincemeat mixture and cherries to ✱ below. Cover and refrigerate in separate containers. Up to 2 hours in advance, assemble parfaits as directed right.

Place pudding mix in 4-cup measure. Blend in milk. Microwave at High for 6 to 9 minutes, or until mixture thickens and bubbles, stirring after the first 3 minutes and then every minute.

Place plastic wrap directly on surface of pudding. Refrigerate about 4 hours, or until completely cool.

Combine mincemeat and rum extract in small mixing bowl. Set aside. Reserve 8 whole cherries for garnish. Set aside. Coarsely chop remaining cherries. ✱ Fold 2 cups whipped topping into cold pudding.

Layer ¼ cup pudding mixture, ¼ cup mincemeat mixture, scant 1 tablespoon chopped cherries and ¼ cup pudding mixture in each of eight 8-oz. parfait or wine glasses.

Garnish each parfait with a dollop of remaining whipped topping and a whole cherry before serving.

Pumpkin Cheesecake

Crust:

¼ cup butter or margarine
1 cup graham cracker crumbs
2 tablespoons sugar

Filling:

2 pkgs. (8 oz. each) cream cheese
1 cup canned pumpkin
4 eggs
⅔ cup sugar
1 teaspoon imitation brandy extract
¼ teaspoon ground cinnamon
¼ teaspoon ground ginger
¼ teaspoon ground nutmeg

Topping:

½ cup sour cream
2 tablespoons powdered sugar
¼ teaspoon imitation brandy extract

8 to 10 servings

In 9-inch round baking dish, microwave butter at High for 1¼ to 1½ minutes, or until melted. Stir in graham cracker crumbs and sugar. Mix well. Press mixture firmly against bottom of dish. Microwave at High for 1½ to 2 minutes, or until set, rotating dish once. Set aside.

In 8-cup measure, microwave cream cheese at 50% (Medium) for 2¼ to 4 minutes, or until softened. Add remaining filling ingredients. Beat at medium speed of electric mixer until well blended. Microwave at High for 4 to 5 minutes, or until mixture is very hot and starts to set, beating with whisk every 2 minutes.

Pour filling over prepared crust. Place dish on saucer in microwave oven. Microwave at 50% (Medium) for 7 to 15 minutes, or until center is almost set, rotating dish twice. (Filling becomes firm as it cools.) Chill 1 hour.

In small mixing bowl, combine topping ingredients. Stir until smooth. Spread topping over cheesecake. Refrigerate at least 8 hours, or overnight.

Pistachio-Cherry Cheesecake

Crust:
¼ cup butter or margarine
1 cup finely crushed chocolate wafer crumbs (about 20 wafers)

Filling:
1 pkg. (6 oz.) white baking bar
2 pkgs. (8 oz. each) cream cheese
⅔ cup sugar
2 egg whites
1 tablespoon all-purpose flour
1 teaspoon vanilla
½ cup chopped pistachio nuts
½ cup chopped candied cherries

8 to 10 servings

In 9-inch round baking dish, microwave butter at High for 1¼ to 1½ minutes, or until melted. Stir in wafer crumbs. Mix well. Press mixture firmly against bottom of dish. Microwave at High for 1½ to 2 minutes, or until set, rotating dish once. Set aside.

In small mixing bowl, microwave baking bar at 50% (Medium) for 4 to 5 minutes, or until bar melts and can be stirred smooth, stirring after the first 2 minutes and then every minute. Set aside.

In 2-quart measure, microwave cream cheese at 50% (Medium) for 2¼ to 4 minutes, or until softened. Blend in melted baking bar. Add remaining filling ingredients, except pistachios and cherries. Beat at medium speed of electric mixer until well blended. Microwave at High for 2 minutes, or until mixture starts to set, beating with whisk every minute. Stir in pistachios and cherries.

Pour filling over prepared crust. Place dish on saucer in microwave oven. Microwave at 50% (Medium) for 7 to 10 minutes, or until cheesecake is set in center, rotating dish twice. (Filling becomes firm as it cools.) Refrigerate at least 8 hours, or overnight. Garnish with whole candied cherries, if desired.

Advance preparation: Up to 2 days in advance, prepare as directed above. Cover with plastic wrap and refrigerate.

Mint-Strawberry Cheesecake

1 frozen plain cheesecake (17 to 23 oz.), defrosted (below)
1 square (1 oz.) semisweet chocolate
1 teaspoon shortening
¼ cup mint jelly
2 drops green food coloring
2 teaspoons light corn syrup, divided
¼ cup strawberry jelly
2 drops red food coloring

8 servings

Advance preparation: Up to 1 hour in advance, prepare as directed below.

How to Defrost Cheesecake

How to Microwave Mint-Strawberry Cheesecake

Unwrap cheesecake. Remove from foil pan and place on serving plate or platter. Microwave at 30% (Medium Low) for 2½ to 4 minutes, or until wooden pick inserted in center meets no resistance, rotating plate once or twice. Let cheesecake stand for 10 minutes to complete defrosting.

Place chocolate and shortening in small bowl. Microwave at 50% (Medium) for 2½ to 4½ minutes, or until chocolate is glossy and can be stirred smooth. Place melted chocolate in 1-quart sealable freezer bag. Using scissors, snip corner to form writing tip. Use melted chocolate to pipe outline of design on cheesecake.

Place mint jelly, green food coloring and 1 teaspoon corn syrup in small bowl. Microwave at High for 45 seconds to 1 minute, or until melted. Repeat with strawberry jelly, red food coloring and remaining 1 teaspoon corn syrup. Fill center of chocolate design with melted jellies.

Snowflake Cheesecake ▶

1 frozen plain cheesecake (17 to 23 oz.), defrosted (opposite)
1 doily (6 inch)
  Red and green colored sugar
1 pkg. (3 oz.) cream cheese (optional)
2 to 3 drops green food coloring (optional)

8 servings

Place doily on top of cheesecake. Sprinkle with sugars. Remove doily. In small bowl, microwave cream cheese at High for 15 to 30 seconds, or until softened. Stir in food coloring. Place cream cheese mixture in pastry bag and pipe around edges of cheese-cake to decorate.

Advance preparation: Up to 1 hour in advance, prepare as directed above.

Peppermint Cheesecake ▶

1 frozen plain cheesecake (17 to 23 oz.), defrosted (opposite)
3 tablespoons crushed peppermint candies
1 square (1 oz.) semisweet chocolate
1 teaspoon shortening

8 servings

Sprinkle peppermint candies over top of cheesecake. In small bowl, microwave chocolate and shortening at 50% (Medium) for 2 to 3 minutes, or until chocolate is glossy and can be stirred smooth. Using spoon, drizzle chocolate over top of candies and cheesecake. Chill until chocolate is set.

Advance preparation: Up to 1 hour in advance, prepare as directed above.

Easy Yule Log Cake

2 frozen chocolate layer cakes
　　(11½ oz. each)
⅓ cup butter or margarine
1¾ to 2 cups powdered sugar
⅔ cup cocoa
⅓ cup half-and-half
1 teaspoon vanilla
1 pkg. (3 oz.) cream cheese
2 teaspoons granulated sugar
4 drops yellow food coloring
3 drops red food coloring
1 drop green food coloring
　 Spearmint gumdrop leaves
　 Red cinnamon candies

8 to 10 servings

Advance preparation: Up to
1 day in advance, prepare as
directed right. Cover and
refrigerate.

How to Microwave Easy Yule Log Cake

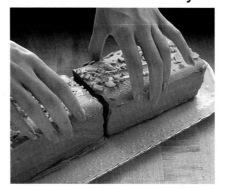

Unwrap cakes and place end to
end on serving platter. Set aside.
In large mixing bowl, microwave
butter at 30% (Medium Low) for
45 seconds to 1 minute, or until
softened, checking every 15 to
30 seconds.

Beat butter at medium speed of
electric mixer until creamed. Add
powdered sugar and cocoa alternately with half-and-half while
beating at medium speed of
electric mixer, until of desired
spreading consistency. Blend in
vanilla. Reserve 2 tablespoons
frosting. Set aside.

Spread top and sides of cake with remaining frosting. Draw tines of fork through frosting for barklike appearance of log. Set log aside.

Place cream cheese in small bowl. Microwave at High for 15 to 30 seconds, or until softened. Add granulated sugar and food colorings. Mix well.

Spread ends of log with cream cheese mixture. Use wooden pick to apply reserved frosting in concentric circles on each end of log. Garnish log with gumdrop leaves and red cinnamon candies.

Raspberry Ice Cream Cake

- 1 frozen pound cake (16 oz.)
- 1 pint raspberry sherbet
- 1 pint chocolate ice cream
- 1 square (1 oz.) semisweet chocolate
- ½ teaspoon shortening
- ½ cup raspberry preserves
- 2 teaspoons light corn syrup
- Fresh raspberries (optional)

8 servings

Advance preparation: Up to 1 week in advance, prepare cake to ✳ below. To serve, prepare raspberry sauce and continue as directed.

How to Microwave Raspberry Ice Cream Cake

Cut pound cake lengthwise into thirds. Place bottom cake layer on serving platter. Set aside. Remove covers from sherbet and ice cream. Microwave sherbet at 50% (Medium) for 30 seconds to 1 minute, or until softened. Repeat with ice cream.

Spread bottom cake layer with about 1 cup of the raspberry sherbet. Top with next cake layer. Spread second layer with about ½ cup of the chocolate ice cream. Place remaining cake layer on top.

Spread top with remaining raspberry sherbet. Spread sides with remaining chocolate ice cream. (If sherbet or ice cream becomes too soft, freeze 10 to 15 minutes.) Freeze cake 15 to 30 minutes, or until very firm.

Combine chocolate and shortening in 1-cup measure. Microwave at 50% (Medium) for 1½ to 3 minutes, or until chocolate is glossy and can be stirred smooth, stirring once. Cool slightly.

Drizzle chocolate over top of raspberry sherbet. Freeze uncovered until firm. ✳ To serve, combine raspberry preserves and corn syrup in 1-cup measure. Microwave at 50% (Medium) for 1 minute, or until mixture is melted and can be stirred smooth. Drizzle raspberry sauce over servings of cake. Garnish each serving with fresh raspberries.

Holiday Brunch

Give your brunch an Indian touch with Curried Eggs, or choose the Tex-Mex flavor of Picante Potato Pie. Fruit salad, muffins and assorted butters complete either menu.

Curried Eggs & Muffins

4 English muffins, split and
 toasted
8 hard-cooked eggs, peeled
¼ cup butter or margarine
¼ cup all-purpose flour
2 teaspoons curry powder
½ teaspoon salt
⅛ teaspoon white pepper
2 cups milk

Toppings:
Crumbled cooked bacon
Sliced green onions
Shredded carrot
Chopped nuts
Shredded coconut
Chopped fully cooked ham
Chopped red and green pepper

8 servings

Heat conventional oven to 200°F. Arrange muffin halves on large oven-proof platter. Slice each egg lengthwise into 4 slices. Place 4 egg slices on each toasted muffin half. Cover platter with foil. Place in oven for 15 to 20 minutes.

In 4-cup measure, microwave butter at High for 1¼ to 1½ minutes, or until melted. Stir in flour, curry powder, salt and pepper. Blend in milk. Microwave at High for 7 to 9 minutes, or until sauce thickens and bubbles, stirring twice.

Remove platter from oven. Remove foil. Spoon curry sauce over eggs and muffins. Sprinkle with desired toppings.

Advance preparation: Up to 1 day in advance, cook eggs, but do not peel. Refrigerate. To serve, peel eggs and prepare recipe as directed above.

Butter Spreads ▶ & Warm Quick Breads

Tangy Lime Butter:
½ cup butter or margarine
1 teaspoon grated lime peel
1 tablespoon fresh lime juice

Rum-Walnut Butter:
½ cup butter or margarine
2 tablespoons chopped
 walnuts
¼ teaspoon imitation rum
 extract

Spiced Butter:
½ cup butter or margarine
¼ teaspoon ground allspice

Cherry Butter:
½ cup butter or margarine
1 tablespoon cherry preserves

Quick Breads:
1 pkg. (10 oz.) frozen muffins
 (4 muffins)
1 pkg. (12 oz.) frozen snack
 loaves (6 loaves)

10 servings

In small mixing bowl, microwave butter at 30% (Medium Low) for 15 seconds to 1 minute, or until softened, checking every 15 seconds. Blend in remaining ingredients for desired flavor. ✳

To warm muffins and loaves, arrange in napkin-lined nonmetallic basket. Cover with another napkin. Microwave at High for 2 to 2½ minutes, or until muffins and loaves are warm, rearranging once.

Advance preparation: Up to 2 weeks in advance, prepare as directed to ✳ above. Cover and refrigerate.

Picante Potato Pie ▲

4 cups frozen hash brown
   potato cubes
4 eggs
2 tablespoons all-purpose flour
1 cup finely chopped fully
   cooked ham
1 cup shredded Monterey Jack
   cheese
¾ cup picante sauce
1 can (4 oz.) chopped green
   chilies
¼ cup sliced green onions
¼ teaspoon salt
⅛ teaspoon pepper
½ cup shredded Cheddar
   cheese
1 large tomato, chopped
   (about 1 cup)

8 servings

In 10-inch deep-dish pie plate, microwave potatoes at High for 4 to 6 minutes, or until defrosted, stirring once. Set aside.

In medium mixing bowl, combine remaining ingredients, except Cheddar cheese and tomato. Stir in potatoes. Spoon back into pie plate. Cover with wax paper.

Place pie plate on saucer in microwave oven. Microwave at High for 5 minutes. Stir. Microwave at 50% (Medium) for 10 to 15 minutes longer, or until knife inserted in center comes out clean, stirring once.

Sprinkle Cheddar cheese around edge of pie. Microwave at High for 30 to 45 seconds, or until cheese melts. Sprinkle tomato in center of pie. Sprinkle with sliced green onions, if desired.

Hot Strawberry Tea

6 cups hot water
4 tea bags
1 pkg. (16 oz.) frozen
    strawberries without syrup
½ cup orange juice
¼ cup sugar
½ teaspoon grated orange peel
⅛ teaspoon ground nutmeg
8 orange slices

8 servings

Place water in 8-cup measure. Cover with plastic wrap. Microwave at High for 10 to 14 minutes, or until boiling. Add tea bags. Let stand, covered, for 5 minutes. Remove tea bags. Re-cover.

Reserve 4 frozen strawberries. In 2-quart casserole, combine remaining strawberries and remaining ingredients, except orange slices. Cover. Microwave at High for 10 to 14 minutes, or until boiling, stirring once.

Place strawberry mixture in strainer. Press liquid through strainer into medium mixing bowl. Discard pulp. Add strained mixture to tea. Stir gently.

Cut each reserved strawberry into 4 slices. Garnish each serving with 2 strawberry slices and 1 orange slice. To serve cold, chill at least 2 hours and serve over ice.

Hot Raspberry Tea: Follow recipe above, except substitute 1 pkg. (12 oz.) frozen raspberries for strawberries, and decrease sugar to 2 tablespoons. Reserve 16 frozen raspberries. Garnish each serving with 2 raspberries and 1 orange slice.

Winter Salad with Tart Cinnamon Dressing ▲

Salad:
4 cups leaf lettuce, torn into
    bite-size pieces
3 medium oranges, peeled and
    sectioned
2 medium pears, sliced
1 avocado, peeled and sliced
    Pomegranate seeds (optional)

Dressing:
½ cup olive oil
3 tablespoons apple juice
2 tablespoons sugar
1 tablespoon vinegar
1 teaspoon ground cinnamon
½ teaspoon dry mustard

8 servings

In large mixing bowl, combine all salad ingredients, except pomegranate seeds.✴ Set aside. In blender, combine all dressing ingredients. Blend for about 30 to 45 seconds, or until smooth. Pour dressing over salad. Toss gently to coat. Sprinkle with pomegranate seeds. Serve immediately.

Advance preparation: Up to 2 hours in advance, dip pear and avocado slices in lemon juice to prevent browning. Prepare salad mixture to ✴ above. Cover and refrigerate. To serve, continue as directed.

Bowl Games

*Holiday-season bowl games have become important occasions
for casual entertaining. Offer foods for nibbling — like the
Cheese & Garlic-flavored Nuts or Mexican Chili Dip — and for
more serious eating — like the hearty Layered Buffet Sandwich
and Crunchy Cabbage Salad. Satisfy a sweet tooth with
Bowl Game Brownies and Fudgy Popcorn.*

Layered Buffet Sandwich

1 loaf (1 lb.) French bread	Lettuce
1 cup chopped green pepper	⅓ lb. fully cooked turkey, thinly sliced
½ cup chopped red onion	¼ lb. salami, thinly sliced
2 tablespoons butter or margarine	⅓ lb. fully cooked ham, thinly sliced
2 cups sliced fresh mushrooms	6 slices (1 oz. each) Provolone cheese
¼ cup olive oil	6 slices (¾ oz. each) pasteurized process American cheese
¼ cup cider vinegar	
1 teaspoon Dijon mustard	
½ teaspoon sugar	
¼ teaspoon Italian seasoning	
¼ teaspoon salt	

6 to 8 servings

Slice French bread in half lengthwise. Set aside. In 1½-quart casserole,
combine green pepper, onion and butter. Cover. Microwave at High for
2 minutes. Stir in mushrooms. Re-cover. Microwave at High for 3 to 5 minutes, or until green pepper and onion are tender-crisp. Drain. Set aside.
In small bowl, combine oil, vinegar, mustard, sugar, Italian seasoning and
salt. Blend well with whisk. Microwave at High for 30 seconds to 1 minute, or until mixture boils. Brush oil mixture evenly over cut sides of loaf.

Arrange lettuce evenly over bottom half of loaf. Top with turkey and
salami. Spoon drained vegetables over salami. Top with remaining ingredients. Place top of loaf over cheeses. Press lightly. ✳ Wrap in plastic
wrap and chill at least 2 hours. Cut diagonally into serving-size pieces.
Secure each piece with wooden pick.

Advance preparation: Up to 24 hours in advance, prepare to ✳
above. Wrap in plastic wrap and refrigerate. To serve, cut and secure
with wooden picks as directed.

Fiery Chicken Wings & Dipping Sauce ▶

3 lbs. chicken wings
⅓ cup all-purpose flour
  Vegetable oil
2 teaspoons paprika
1 teaspoon garlic salt
½ teaspoon coarsely ground
  pepper

Sauce:
2 tablespoons finely chopped
  onion

2 teaspoons vegetable oil
1 can (8 oz.) tomato sauce
1 tablespoon packed brown
  sugar
2 teaspoons cider vinegar
1 teaspoon paprika
¼ teaspoon coarsely ground
  pepper
¼ teaspoon garlic salt
⅛ teaspoon cayenne

10 to 12 servings

Advance preparation: Up to 1 day in advance, prepare as directed to ✳ below. Cover and refrigerate chicken and sauce in separate containers. To serve, place half of chicken wings on paper-towel-lined plate. Microwave at High for 3 to 4 minutes, or until hot, rotating plate once. Repeat for remaining wings. Microwave sauce at High for 2 to 3 minutes, or until hot, stirring once. Serve sauce with wings.

How to Make Fiery Chicken Wings & Dipping Sauce

Separate each chicken wing into 3 parts, cutting at joints. Discard wing tips. Place flour and wing pieces in large plastic food-storage bag. Shake to coat.

Heat ¼ inch oil in deep 10-inch skillet conventionally over medium-high heat. Fry half of chicken wings at a time for 6 to 8 minutes, or until golden brown, turning once or twice. Drain on paper towel. Set aside.

Combine 2 teaspoons paprika, 1 teaspoon garlic salt and ½ teaspoon pepper in small bowl. Sprinkle evenly over wings. Set aside.

Crunchy Cabbage Salad

3 cups shredded green
   cabbage
3 cups shredded red cabbage
1 cup shredded carrot
⅓ cup salted blanched peanuts
   (optional)
2 green onions, thinly sliced
1 package (3 oz.) chicken-
   flavored Oriental dry noodle
   soup mix

Dressing:
¼ cup vegetable oil
3 tablespoons red wine vinegar
2 tablespoons sugar
¼ teaspoon salt
¼ teaspoon pepper

8 servings

In large mixing bowl, combine cabbages, carrot, peanuts and onions. Sprinkle dry soup seasoning packet over salad. Break dry noodles into small pieces and add to salad. Mix well.

In 1-cup measure, combine all dressing ingredients. Mix well. Pour over salad, tossing gently to coat.

Advance preparation: Up to 4 hours in advance, prepare as directed above. (If softer noodles are desired, prepare salad up to 24 hours in advance.) Cover and refrigerate.

Combine onion and 2 teaspoons oil in 1-quart casserole. Microwave at High for 1 to 2 minutes, or until tender. Stir in remaining ingredients. Microwave at High for 5 to 7 minutes, or until slightly thickened, stirring twice. ✳ Serve with wings.

Mexican Chili Dip

1 cup chopped red pepper
1 cup chopped green pepper
1 pkg. (3 oz.) cream cheese
1 cup sour cream
⅛ teaspoon cayenne

1 can (15 oz.) red kidney beans in chili gravy
1 cup shredded Monterey Jack cheese
½ cup shredded Cheddar cheese

1 pkg. (6 oz.) frozen avocado guacamole, defrosted
1 cup seeded chopped tomato
Round tortilla chips

8 servings

How to Microwave Mexican Chili Dip

Combine red and green peppers in 1-quart casserole. Cover. Microwave at High for 4 to 5 minutes, or until tender-crisp, stirring once. Cool slightly.

Place cream cheese in small bowl. Microwave at High for 15 to 30 seconds, or until softened. Blend in sour cream and cayenne until smooth.

Spoon cream cheese mixture around bottom edge of 10-inch deep-dish pie plate, forming ring about 1½ inches wide.

Spoon kidney beans in center and slightly over cream cheese mixture. Sprinkle evenly with peppers. Cover with wax paper. Microwave at 50% (Medium) for 6 to 8 minutes, or until warm in center, rotating dish once.

Sprinkle Monterey Jack cheese in circle around edge. Sprinkle Cheddar cheese in center. Cover with wax paper. Microwave at High for 1 to 3 minutes, or until cheese melts.

Spoon guacamole on top in wreath shape. Sprinkle tomatoes in center and around guacamole wreath. Place tortilla chips upright around edge of dish.

Cheese & Garlic-flavored Nuts

2 tablespoons butter or
  margarine
2 teaspoons Worcestershire
  sauce
1 teaspoon garlic salt
½ cup whole blanched almonds
½ cup whole salted cashews
½ cup pecan halves
½ cup unsalted dry roasted
  peanuts
1 tablespoon grated Parmesan
  cheese

2 cups

In 2-quart casserole, microwave butter at High for 45 seconds to 1 minute, or until melted. Add Worcestershire sauce and garlic salt. Mix well. Add nuts, stirring to coat. Microwave at High for 6 to 9 minutes, or until butter is absorbed, stirring 2 or 3 times. Add Parmesan cheese. Toss to coat. Spread on paper-towel-lined baking sheet to cool.

Advance preparation: Up to 1 week in advance, prepare as directed above. Store in airtight container.

Fudgy Popcorn ▲

10 cups popped popcorn
½ cup butter or margarine
½ cup packed brown sugar
¼ cup cocoa
2 tablespoons light corn syrup

10 cups

Heat conventional oven to 325°F. Place popcorn in large mixing bowl. Set aside. In small mixing bowl, microwave butter at High for 1½ to 1¾ minutes, or until melted. Add remaining ingredients. Mix well.

Pour butter mixture over popcorn. Toss gently to coat. Spread coated popcorn in an even layer in 15½ × 10½-inch jelly roll pan. Bake for 10 minutes, stirring twice. Watch closely to prevent burning.

Advance preparation: Up to 1 week in advance, prepare as directed above. Store in airtight container.

Bowl Game Brownies

1 pkg. (21.5 to 23.6 oz.) fudge
brownie mix

Frosting:

⅓ cup butter or margarine
1¾ to 2 cups powdered sugar
⅔ cup cocoa
⅓ cup half-and-half
1 teaspoon vanilla
1 square (2 oz.) white candy
coating

2 dozen brownies

Heat conventional oven to 350°F.
Grease 15½ × 10½-inch jelly roll
pan. Set aside. Prepare brownies
according to package directions.
Spread evenly in prepared jelly
roll pan. Bake for 10 to 17 minutes, or until set and dry on top.
Let cool for 2 hours.

In large mixing bowl, microwave butter at 30% (Medium
Low) for 45 seconds to 1 minute,
or until softened, checking every
15 to 30 seconds. Beat butter at
medium speed of electric mixer
until creamed.

Add powdered sugar and cocoa
alternately with half-and-half
while beating at medium speed
of electric mixer until of desired
consistency. Blend in vanilla.
Spread top of brownies with frosting. Using sharp knife, cut brownies diagonally every 1½ inches in
diamond pattern. Melt candy coating and decorate brownies (right).

Advance preparation: Up to
1 day in advance, prepare as
directed above. Store in airtight
container.

How to Decorate Bowl Game Brownies

Place candy coating in small
mixing bowl. Microwave at 50%
(Medium) for 3 to 4 minutes,
or until coating can be stirred
smooth. Spoon into 1-quart sealable freezer bag.

Squeeze coating to one corner
of bag. Seal bag. Using scissors,
snip corner of bag slightly to
form writing tip. Pipe football
laces on each brownie.

Winter Warm-Ups

*Outdoor activities — caroling, skating, sledding, sleighing —
call for something piping hot when participants pull off their mittens
and shake the snow from their boots.*

Rich Almond Hot Chocolate

- 4 squares (1 oz. each) semisweet chocolate
- 2 tablespoons butter or margarine
- 1 can (14 oz.) sweetened condensed milk
- 4 cups milk
- ½ teaspoon almond extract

4 to 6 servings

In 8-cup measure, microwave chocolate and butter at 50% (Medium) for 3½ to 4½ minutes, or until chocolate is glossy and mixture can be stirred smooth. Add condensed milk. Mix well.

Blend in milk gradually, stirring with whisk after each addition. Microwave at High for 9 to 14 minutes, or until mixture is hot, stirring 2 or 3 times. Stir in almond extract. Top each serving with miniature marshmallows, if desired.

Hot Buttered Rum

- ⅓ cup butter or margarine
- ¼ teaspoon ground nutmeg
- 4 cups apple juice
- ⅔ to 1 cup dark rum
- ⅓ cup packed brown sugar
  Grated orange peel (optional)

6 to 8 servings

In 8-cup measure, microwave butter and nutmeg at High for 1½ to 1¾ minutes, or until butter melts. Stir in apple juice, rum and brown sugar. Microwave at High for 6 to 9 minutes, or until hot, stirring twice. Top each serving with orange peel.

Hot Spiced Burgundy

- ⅓ cup sugar
- 1 jar (6 oz.) maraschino cherries, undrained
- 4 cups Burgundy wine
- 1 large orange
- 1 large lemon
- 6 whole cloves
- 6 whole allspice

6 to 8 servings

Place sugar in 8-cup measure. Add cherries with juice. Stir in wine. Set aside.

Cut 4 thin slices each from orange and lemon. Add slices to wine mixture. Squeeze juices from remaining portion of orange and lemon. Add juice to wine mixture. Stir in cloves and allspice. Microwave at High for 9 to 12 minutes, or until hot, stirring twice.

Mixed Fruit Warmer ▶

- 1 can (6 oz.) frozen orange juice concentrate
- 1 bottle (32 oz.) cranberry-raspberry drink
- 2 cups water
- ⅓ cup packed brown sugar
- 4 thin orange slices
- 1 small cinnamon stick

6 to 8 servings

Remove metal lid from one end of orange juice. Place orange juice in microwave oven. Microwave at High for 45 seconds to 1 minute, or until defrosted. Pour into 8-cup measure.

Stir in cranberry-raspberry drink, water and brown sugar. Add orange slices and cinnamon stick. Microwave at High for 11 to 16 minutes, or until hot, stirring once or twice. Before serving, remove cinnamon stick.

◄ Melted Cheese Bread

Cheese Mixture:

1½ cups shredded mozzarella
    cheese
1½ cups shredded Colby
    cheese
 ½ teaspoon garlic salt
 ½ teaspoon Italian seasoning

 ¼ cup butter or margarine
 2 tablespoons Italian dressing
 2 tablespoons olive oil
 1 loaf (1 lb.) French bread,
    sliced diagonally
    (1-inch slices)

6 to 8 servings

In medium mixing bowl, combine all cheese mixture ingredients. Toss to coat. Set aside.✳
In 1-quart casserole, combine butter, Italian dressing and oil. Microwave at High for 1 to 1¼ minutes, or until butter melts. Brush butter mixture on one side of each bread slice.

To microwave, arrange 4 slices bread buttered-side-up on paper-towel-lined plate. Sprinkle each with about ¼ cup of the cheese mixture. Microwave at High for 1¾ to 2½ minutes, or until cheeses melt, rotating plate once. Repeat with remaining bread slices.

To conventionally bake, arrange bread slices buttered-side-up on baking sheet. Sprinkle each with about ¼ cup of the cheese mixture. Place under conventional broiler, 2 to 3 inches from heat. Broil until cheeses melt and begin to brown.

Advance preparation: Up to 1 day in advance, prepare as directed to ✳ above. Cover and refrigerate. To serve, continue as directed.

Quick Chicken Vegetable Soup ▲

4 cups hot water
2 cans (10¾ oz. each)
    condensed chicken
    noodle soup

1 pkg. (10 oz.) frozen mixed
    vegetables in butter sauce
1 cup cubed cooked chicken or
    turkey (½-inch cubes)

6 to 8 servings

In 3-quart casserole, combine all ingredients. Cover. Microwave at High for 14 to 20 minutes, or until vegetables are tender and soup is hot, stirring twice.

Creamy Salmon Soup ▶

¼ cup butter or margarine
¼ cup sliced green onions
½ teaspoon grated lemon peel
½ teaspoon dried marjoram
　 leaves
¼ cup all-purpose flour
½ teaspoon salt
⅛ teaspoon white pepper
3 cups milk
1 pkg. (8 oz.) cream cheese
2 cans (6½ oz. each) skinless,
　 boneless salmon, drained
1½ cups frozen peas
1 jar (2 oz.) sliced pimiento,
　 drained, divided

6 to 8 servings

In 3-quart casserole, combine butter, onions, lemon peel and marjoram. Cover. Microwave at High for 2½ to 4 minutes, or until onions are tender. Stir in flour, salt and pepper. Blend in milk. Microwave at High for 9 to 11 minutes, or until mixture thickens and bubbles, stirring 2 or 3 times with whisk.

In small bowl, microwave cream cheese at 50% (Medium) for 1½ to 3 minutes, or until softened. Add to milk mixture. Beat well with whisk until smooth. Stir in remaining ingredients, reserving 1 tablespoon pimiento. Cover. Microwave at High for 3 to 5 minutes, or until hot.✳ Garnish each serving with reserved pimiento.

Advance preparation: Up to 24 hours in advance, prepare as directed to ✳ above. Cover and refrigerate soup and reserved pimiento in separate containers. To serve, microwave soup at High for 10 to 13 minutes, or until hot, stirring once. Garnish each serving with reserved pimiento.

Crab-Tomato Bisque

¾ cup white wine
¼ cup finely chopped celery
¼ cup finely chopped carrot
¼ cup finely chopped leek
2 tablespoons butter or
　 margarine
¼ teaspoon ground thyme
3 tablespoons tomato paste
2 cans (14½ oz. each) ready-to-
　 serve chicken broth

2 cans (6 oz. each) crabmeat,
　 rinsed, drained and
　 cartilage removed
1¼ cups half-and-half
1¼ cups instant mashed potato
　 flakes
½ teaspoon salt
　 Dash to ⅛ teaspoon
　 cayenne
1 small tomato, seeded and
　 chopped
　 Snipped fresh parsley

6 to 8 servings

In 3-quart casserole, combine wine, celery, carrot, leek, butter and thyme. Cover. Microwave at High for 8 to 12 minutes, or until vegetables are tender, stirring once. Let mixture stand, covered, for 5 minutes.

Place mixture in food processor or blender. Add tomato paste. Process until smooth. Return mixture to casserole. Stir in remaining ingredients, except tomato and parsley. Cover.✳ Microwave at High for 10 to 16 minutes, or until hot and slightly thickened, stirring 2 or 3 times. Before serving, sprinkle with tomato and parsley.

Advance preparation: Up to 1 day in advance, prepare as directed to ✳ above. Refrigerate. To serve, continue as directed.

Holiday Open House

To encourage mingling at your Open House, provide small plates for foods served buffet style, and distribute dips around the room.

Sparkling Grape Punch with Fruit Ice Ring

2 cups crushed ice

4 small clusters seedless green grapes

1 cup frozen whole cranberries

1 kiwifruit, peeled and sliced crosswise (¼ inch thick)

4 slices orange (¼ inch thick)

1 bottle (64 oz.) cranberry juice cocktail, divided

1 bottle (25 oz.) nonalcoholic sparkling grape juice, chilled

Sixteen 6-oz. servings

How to Make Sparkling Grape Punch with Fruit Ice Ring

Place ice in 6-cup ring mold. Arrange fruits over ice. Pour 2 cups cranberry juice cocktail over fruit. Refrigerate remaining cranberry juice cocktail. Freeze ring at least 8 hours, or overnight.

Dip mold into warm water for 10 to 15 seconds. Carefully unmold and place ice ring fruit-side-up in punch bowl. Add remaining cranberry juice cocktail and the sparkling grape juice.

Shrimp Piquant ▲

1 can (14½ oz.) diced peeled
   tomatoes
1 cup picante sauce
½ cup sliced green onions
1 teaspoon sugar
¼ teaspoon dried thyme
   leaves
1½ lbs. large shrimp, shelled
   and deveined

8 servings

In 2-quart casserole, combine all ingredients, except shrimp. Cover. Microwave at High for 8 to 12 minutes, or until onions are tender-crisp, stirring 2 or 3 times. Stir in shrimp. Re-cover. Microwave at High for 4½ to 6½ minutes, or until shrimp are opaque, stirring once. Refrigerate at least 12 hours. Serve cold with wooden picks.

Turkey Pâté Truffles ▲

2 slices soft whole wheat bread
¾ cup chopped pecans
1 large apple, cored, peeled
   and chopped (about 1 cup)
½ cup chopped onion
½ cup chopped carrot
2 pkgs. (8 oz. each) cream
   cheese

2 cups chopped cooked turkey
1 tablespoon Dijon mustard
½ teaspoon salt
½ teaspoon dried tarragon
   leaves
⅛ teaspoon pepper

3½ to 4 dozen truffles

In food processor, place bread and pecans. Process until fine. Place mixture in small mixing bowl. Set aside.

In 1-quart casserole, combine apple, onion and carrot. Cover. Microwave at High for 5 to 7 minutes, or until mixture is very tender, stirring once. Cool 10 minutes. Place in food processor. Add remaining ingredients, except bread crumb mixture. Process until smooth. Place mixture in medium mixing bowl. Cover with plastic wrap. Chill at least 4 hours, or until firm. Form mixture into ¾ to 1-inch balls. Roll each in bread crumb mixture. Place on wax-paper-lined baking sheet. Cover with plastic wrap.✳ Chill at least 4 hours.

Advance preparation: Up to 24 hours in advance, prepare truffles to ✳ above. Refrigerate.

Marinated Tortellini & Broccoli Appetizer

1 pkg. (10 to 12 oz.) fresh
   uncooked tortellini (about
   3 cups)
⅓ cup white wine vinegar
⅓ cup olive oil
½ teaspoon grated lemon peel
1 tablespoon fresh lemon juice
1 teaspoon sugar
½ teaspoon salt
¼ teaspoon dried basil leaves
4 cups fresh broccoli flowerets
   or cauliflowerets
2 cups cherry tomatoes

8 servings

Prepare tortellini as directed on package. Rinse with cold water. Drain. Set aside. In 2-quart casserole, combine remaining ingredients, except broccoli and tomatoes. Mix well. Stir in broccoli. Cover. Microwave at High for 3 to 5½ minutes, or until tender-crisp.

Add tortellini. Toss to coat. Re-cover. Chill at least 4 hours. Stir in tomatoes. Serve skewered on 3-inch wooden picks.

Advance preparation: Up to 24 hours in advance, prepare as directed above. Cover and refrigerate.

Buffet Meatballs

Meatballs:

1½	lbs. ground veal
½	lb. ground turkey
2	eggs
1	cup soft bread crumbs
½	cup apple juice
¼	cup finely chopped onion
2	tablespoons snipped fresh parsley
¾	teaspoon salt
¾	teaspoon ground coriander
¼	teaspoon dried thyme leaves
¼	teaspoon pepper

Sauce:

2	carrots, diagonally sliced (½ inch thick)
2	tablespoons butter or margarine
1	tablespoon snipped fresh parsley
1	cup ready-to-serve beef broth
½	cup apple juice
2	tablespoons cornstarch
¾	teaspoon ground coriander
½	teaspoon salt
⅛	teaspoon pepper

10 to 12 servings

Heat conventional oven to 350°F. Lightly grease 15½ × 10½-inch jelly roll pan. Set aside. In large mixing bowl, combine all meatball ingredients. Mix well. Shape into ninety ¾-inch meatballs. Arrange in even layer in prepared pan. Bake for 12 to 15 minutes, or until light golden brown. Drain. Cover loosely with foil to keep warm. Set aside✳.

In 1½-quart casserole, combine carrots, butter and parsley. Cover. Microwave at High for 2 to 3 minutes, or until butter melts. Add beef broth. Set aside.

In 1-cup measure, blend apple juice and cornstarch. Blend into broth mixture. Stir in coriander, salt and pepper. Microwave at High for 7 to 10 minutes, or until sauce is thickened and translucent, stirring 3 or 4 times. Set aside.

Place meatballs in 10-inch square casserole. Add sauce. Toss to coat. Garnish with green pepper chunks, if desired. Serve with wooden picks.

Advance preparation: Up to 2 days in advance, prepare as directed to ✳ above. Cover and refrigerate meatballs. To serve, continue as directed, except microwave meatballs at High for 9 to 15 minutes, or until hot, stirring 2 or 3 times.

◀ Red Pepper Dip

Red Pepper Dip

- 2 large red peppers
- 1 cup sour cream
- 2 pkgs. (3 oz. each) cream cheese
- ¼ teaspoon salt
- ¼ teaspoon paprika
- ⅛ teaspoon cayenne

2½ cups

Cut peppers in half lengthwise. Remove stem, seeds and membrane. Place peppers cut-side-down in 9-inch square baking dish. Cover with plastic wrap. Microwave at High for 8 to 10 minutes, or until tender, rearranging pepper halves once. Place peppers in cold water. Remove and discard skins. Drain skinned pepper halves on paper towel.

In food processor or blender, combine peppers and remaining ingredients. Process until smooth. Refrigerate at least 12 hours. Serve with fresh vegetables and bagel chips.

Lemon Brie Dip

- 2 wheels (8 oz. each) Brie cheese
- ⅔ cup whipping cream
- ½ teaspoon grated lemon peel
- ½ cup sliced almonds, divided
  Red and green apple slices
  Pear slices
  Red and green seedless grapes
  French bread cubes

2 cups

Cut rind from Brie. Discard rind. Place Brie in 2-quart casserole or serving dish. Add whipping cream and lemon peel. Microwave at 50% (Medium) for 4 to 6 minutes, or until Brie is melted and mixture can be stirred smooth, stirring after every minute.

Reserve 1 tablespoon almonds for garnish. Add remaining almonds to dip. Mix well. Pour into serving dish. Sprinkle reserved almonds on top. Serve with fresh fruit and French bread as dippers.

Italian Flag Dip

- 1 cup finely chopped green pepper
- 1 cup finely chopped mushrooms
- 2 cups shredded mozzarella cheese
- ¼ cup grated Parmesan cheese
- 2 teaspoons dried parsley flakes
- ¾ cup pizza sauce
- ½ cup finely chopped pepperoni (about 2 oz.)

10 to 12 servings

In 1-quart clear glass casserole or serving dish, combine green pepper and mushrooms. Cover with plastic wrap. Microwave at High for 3 to 4 minutes, or until tender, stirring once. Drain, pressing to remove excess moisture. Spread vegetables evenly in dish. Set aside.

In small mixing bowl, combine cheeses and parsley. Layer one-half of the cheese mixture over vegetables. Spoon pizza sauce evenly over cheeses. Top with pepperoni. Sprinkle with remaining cheese mixture. Microwave at 70% (Medium High) for 5½ to 8 minutes, or until cheeses melt, rotating dish once. Serve with crisp bread sticks.

Roasted Garlic Spread

1 whole bulb garlic (2-inch diameter)
 Olive oil
2 pkgs. (8 oz. each) cream cheese
½ cup mayonnaise
1 jar (2 oz.) sliced pimiento, drained
2 teaspoons freeze-dried chives

2½ cups

Advance preparation: Up to 2 days in advance, prepare as directed below. Cover and refrigerate. Serve with crackers or crisp bread sticks.

How to Make Roasted Garlic Spread

Heat conventional oven to 400°F. Lightly brush outside of garlic bulb with oil. Place in shallow baking pan. Roast on center rack for 30 minutes. Set aside to cool.

Place cream cheese in medium mixing bowl. Microwave at 50% (Medium) for 3½ to 4½ minutes, or until softened. Add remaining ingredients. Mix well. Set aside.

Remove and discard peel from garlic cloves. Mash garlic, using fork. Add to cream cheese mixture. Mix well. Cover and chill at least 4 hours. Serve with crackers or crisp bread sticks.

Dessert Buffet

*The dessert buffet is a festive and flexible way to entertain.
For eight to ten people, select two or three desserts to provide variety.
As your guest list grows, plan another dessert for every eight people.
Arrange the desserts on your dining table, reserving one end
or a separate table to feature the dessert fondue. Choose
one fondue recipe for a small group or all three for a crowd.
A coffee buffet completes the party.*

Cherry Chocolate Fondue

2 pkgs. (6 oz. each) white baking bars, broken up	¼ cup whipping cream
1 cup miniature marshmallows	2 tablespoons cherry-flavored liqueur (optional)
¼ cup maraschino cherry juice	2 drops red food coloring

2 cups

In 1½-quart casserole or serving dish, combine all ingredients, except liqueur and food coloring. Microwave at 50% (Medium) for 5 to 9 minutes, or until baking bars are melted and mixture can be stirred smooth, beating with whisk 2 or 3 times.

Stir in liqueur and food coloring. Serve with dippers and condiments (right). Reheat by microwaving at 50% (Medium) for 1 to 2 minutes, stirring once, or keep warm by placing in fondue pot over very low heat.

Dark Chocolate Fondue

3 bars (4 oz. each) sweet dark chocolate, broken up	½ cup whipping cream
1 cup miniature marshmallows	2 tablespoons orange-flavored liqueur (optional)

2 cups

In 1½-quart casserole or serving dish, combine all ingredients, except liqueur. Microwave at 50% (Medium) for 4 to 8 minutes, or until chocolate is glossy and mixture can be stirred smooth, beating with whisk 2 or 3 times.

Stir in liqueur. Serve with dippers and condiments (right). Reheat by microwaving at 50% (Medium) for 1 to 2 minutes, stirring once, or keep warm by placing in fondue pot over very low heat.

White Chocolate ▶ Almond Fondue

⅓ cup sliced almonds
2 teaspoons butter or margarine
2 pkgs. (6 oz. each) white baking bars, broken up
1 cup miniature marshmallows
½ cup whipping cream

2 cups

In 9-inch pie plate, place almonds and butter. Microwave at High for 4 to 6 minutes, or just until almonds begin to brown, stirring every 2 minutes. Drain on paper towel. Reserve 1 tablespoon toasted almonds for garnish. Chop remaining almonds. Set aside.

In 1½-quart casserole or serving dish, combine remaining ingredients. Microwave at 50% (Medium) for 5 to 9 minutes, or until baking bars are melted and mixture can be stirred smooth, beating with whisk 2 or 3 times.

Stir in chopped almonds. Sprinkle with reserved sliced almonds. Serve with dippers and condiments (below). Reheat by microwaving at 50% (Medium) for 1 to 2 minutes, stirring once, or keep warm by placing in fondue pot over very low heat.

Fondue Dippers ▶

1 to 2-inch pieces pound cake or angel food cake

Fresh fruits:
Whole strawberries
Banana chunks
Pineapple chunks
Apple or pear slices

Advance preparation: Up to 4 hours in advance, cut cake and fruit. Dip fresh fruit pieces in lemon juice to prevent browning. Arrange fruit on serving platter. Cover with plastic wrap and chill until serving time.

Fondue Condiments ▲

½ cup chopped walnuts,
    pecans, peanuts or
    sunflower nuts
½ cup miniature semisweet
    chocolate chips
½ cup vanilla wafer crumbs
½ cup toasted coconut*
¼ cup chocolate or multicolored
    shot

Sprinkle choice of condiments over fondue-dipped cake chunks or fruit pieces.

*To toast coconut, sprinkle ½ cup flaked coconut evenly in 9-inch pie plate. Microwave at High for 3 to 5 minutes, or until lightly browned, tossing with fork after 1 minute and then every 30 seconds.

Fruit in Honey-Lime Sauce

1½ teaspoons cornstarch
⅛ teaspoon grated lime peel
⅛ teaspoon grated fresh
    gingerroot
2 tablespoons fresh lime juice
⅓ cup honey
2 cups sliced fresh
    strawberries
2 medium bananas, sliced
1 can (11 oz.) mandarin
    orange segments, drained
1 cup seedless green grapes
8 individual sponge cake
    cups
1 star fruit, thinly sliced
    (optional)

8 servings

In 2-cup measure, combine cornstarch, lime peel and gingerroot. Blend in lime juice. Stir until smooth. Stir in honey. Microwave at High for 2 to 3 minutes, or until mixture boils, stirring once. Cover with plastic wrap. ✳ Chill until thickened, at least 1 hour.

To serve, combine remaining ingredients, except cake cups and star fruit, in medium mixing bowl. Pour honey sauce over fruit mixture. Toss gently to coat. Arrange cake cups on serving platter. Spoon fruit mixture evenly over cake cups. Top each with 1 slice star fruit.

Advance preparation: Up to 1 day in advance, make honey sauce to ✳ above. Refrigerate. To serve, continue as directed.

Apricot-glazed Apple Tart ▶

18 slices refrigerated sugar
    cookie dough (⅛-inch
    slices)
2 cups milk
½ cup sugar
3 tablespoons cornstarch
    Pinch salt
2 egg yolks
2 Rome apples, cored and
    thinly sliced
¾ cup apricot preserves
1 tablespoon light corn syrup

8 to 10 servings

Apricot-glazed Blueberry Tart:
Follow recipe above, except substitute 1½ to 2 cups fresh blueberries for apples.

Advance preparation: Up to 2 days in advance, prepare crust. Cover with wax paper and store in cool, dry place. Up to 1 day in advance, prepare pastry cream. Place plastic wrap directly on surface and refrigerate. To serve, continue as directed.

How to Make Apricot-glazed Apple Tart

Heat conventional oven to 350°F. Arrange cookie slices in even layer in bottom of 10-inch tart pan. Press cookie dough gently into bottom and up sides of pan. Bake for 10 minutes, or until golden brown. Let cool.

Combine milk, sugar, cornstarch and salt in 4-cup measure. Mix well. Microwave at High for 6 to 10 minutes, or until mixture thickens and bubbles, stirring with whisk after the first 2 minutes and then every minute.

Stir small amount of hot mixture gradually into egg yolks. Blend egg yolks back into hot mixture. Microwave at High for 30 seconds to 1 minute, or until pastry cream thickens slightly, stirring every 30 seconds. Do not overcook.

Place plastic wrap directly on surface of pastry cream. Let cool. Remove cooled crust from pan and place on serving plate. Set aside. Dip apple slices in lemon juice to prevent browning. Pour pastry cream into crust. Top with apple slices, slightly overlapping.

Combine preserves and corn syrup in small mixing bowl. Microwave at High for 1 to 2 minutes, or until melted. Strain. Discard pulp. Cool glaze and spoon evenly over apples.

Champagne Truffles ▲

12 squares (1 oz. each)
        semisweet chocolate
¼ cup butter or margarine
¾ cup powdered sugar
½ cup champagne
¼ teaspoon ground nutmeg

Coatings:
   Powdered sugar
   Chopped almonds
   Shredded coconut
   Crushed vanilla wafers
   Cocoa

3 to 4 dozen truffles

In 8-cup measure, combine chocolate and butter. Microwave at 50% (Medium) for 4 to 5½ minutes, or until chocolate is glossy and mixture can be stirred smooth, stirring twice.

Stir in ¾ cup powdered sugar, the champagne and nutmeg. Beat at medium speed of electric mixer until smooth and shiny, about 1 minute. Cover with plastic wrap. Chill until firm, 2 to 3 hours.

Place each coating in small bowl. Shape chocolate mixture into ¾-inch balls. Roll balls in desired coating. Chill at least 24 hours.

Advance preparation: Up to 1 week in advance, prepare as directed above. Place in airtight container and refrigerate.

Deluxe Caramel Bars ▲

Bar Mixture:
   1 cup butter or margarine
   1 cup packed brown sugar
  ⅓ cup granulated sugar
   2 eggs
   1 teaspoon vanilla
 3½ cups quick-cooking oats
   1 cup all-purpose flour
  ½ cup chopped pecans
  ¼ cup milk
   1 teaspoon baking soda
  ¾ teaspoon salt

Caramel Filling:
   1 bag (14 oz.) caramels
   1 can (14 oz.) sweetened
        condensed milk

Topping:
  ½ cup drained maraschino
        cherries
   2 squares (1 oz. each)
        semisweet chocolate
   2 teaspoons shortening

40 bars

Grease 13 × 9-inch baking pan. Set aside. Heat conventional oven to 325°F. In large mixing bowl, microwave butter at 30% (Medium Low) for 45 seconds to 1¼ minutes, or until softened, checking every 15 seconds.

Add sugars, eggs and vanilla. Beat at medium speed of electric mixer until mixture is creamed. Stir in remaining bar mixture ingredients. Mix well. Reserve 1½ cups bar mixture. Set aside. Pat remaining bar mixture into bottom of prepared pan. Set aside.

In 1-quart casserole, combine caramel filling ingredients. Microwave at 50% (Medium) for 10 to 15 minutes, or until caramels are melted and mixture can be stirred smooth, stirring 3 times. Spoon evenly over bar mixture in pan. Drop reserved 1½ cups bar mixture by teaspoonfuls randomly over top of caramel. Bake for 25 minutes, or until top is golden brown.

Sprinkle top with cherries. Place chocolate and shortening in 1-cup measure. Microwave at 50% (Medium) for 3 to 4½ minutes, or until chocolate is glossy and mixture can be stirred smooth, stirring once. Drizzle in crisscross pattern over top. Cool completely before cutting.

Advance preparation: Up to 2 days in advance, prepare as directed above. Cover with foil and store in cool, dry place.

Peppermint Petits Fours

1 pkg. (16 oz.) frozen pound cake
⅓ cup strawberry preserves
3 cups granulated sugar
1½ cups hot water
½ teaspoon cream of tartar

1¼ cups powdered sugar
½ teaspoon peppermint extract
1 to 2 drops red food coloring
Crushed peppermint candies
Colored sugar
Fresh strawberry slices

16 servings

Advance preparation: Up to 24 hours in advance, prepare petits fours. If topping with fresh strawberries, place on petits fours just before serving.

How to Microwave Peppermint Petits Fours

Trim crusts from pound cake. Cut cake lengthwise into 4 layers. Spread 1 layer with one-half of the preserves. Top with second layer. Repeat to make 2 double layers. Cut each into eight 2-inch squares (16 total). Set aside.

Combine granulated sugar, water and cream of tartar in 3-quart casserole. Microwave at High for 5 to 7 minutes, or until mixture boils. Stir.

Insert microwave candy thermometer. Microwave at High for 7 to 11 minutes, or until mixture reaches 226°F. Let stand on counter about 1 to 1¼ hours, or until cooled to 110°F. (Do not stir or cool over water.)

Add powdered sugar, peppermint extract and food coloring. Beat at medium speed of electric mixer until smooth.

Use 2 forks to dip each layered pound cake square into frosting, coating all sides. Let excess drip off. Place on wire rack over wax paper. Repeat, dipping each square twice.

Decorate with crushed peppermint candies, colored sugar or strawberry slices. Let stand until set.

Cheesecake Tree

 3 pkgs. (8 oz. each) individual
   frozen cheesecakes
¼ lb. chocolate-flavored candy
   coating
 2 teaspoons shortening
12 maraschino cherries with
   stems
   Green colored sugar

12 servings

Remove cheesecakes from package. Arrange in circle on serving platter. Microwave at 30% (Medium Low) for 2 to 3 minutes, or until wooden pick inserted in center meets no resistance, rotating platter once. Let stand for 10 minutes to complete defrosting. Arrange cheesecakes in shape of Christmas tree.

In 1-cup measure, microwave candy coating and shortening at 50% (Medium) for 2 to 4 minutes, or until mixture is melted and can be stirred smooth, stirring once or twice.

Dip one-half of each cherry into chocolate. Place each dipped cherry on wax paper until chocolate is set. Sprinkle cheesecakes lightly with colored sugar. Top each cheesecake with 1 chocolate-covered cherry.

Cinnamon Coffee Mousse ▶

¾ cup sugar
2 tablespoons cornstarch
2 teaspoons instant coffee
   crystals
¼ teaspoon ground cinnamon
2 cups half-and-half
3 egg yolks, beaten
1 cup whipping cream
   Chocolate curls
   Coffee-flavored candy

8 servings

In 8-cup measure, combine sugar, cornstarch, coffee crystals and cinnamon. Blend in half-and-half. Microwave at High for 6 to 9 minutes, or until mixture thickens, beating with whisk 2 or 3 times.

Stir small amount of hot mixture gradually into egg yolks. Blend egg yolks back into hot mixture. Microwave at High for 30 seconds to 1 minute, or until mixture thickens slightly, stirring every 30 seconds. Place plastic wrap directly on surface of pudding. Chill at least 4 hours.

In medium mixing bowl, beat whipping cream at high speed of electric mixer until soft peaks form. Fold whipped cream into chilled pudding. Spoon evenly into each of 8 individual serving dishes.✳ Garnish with chocolate curls or coffee-flavored candy.

Advance preparation: Up to 2 hours in advance, prepare as directed to ✳ above. Refrigerate. To serve, garnish as directed.

Flavored Coffees

For flavored coffee choices on your buffet, place small bowls of chocolate curls, orange rind and cinnamon sticks to add to individual cups of hot coffee.

For flavoring coffee, offer guests an assortment of liqueurs and alcohols, such as orange liqueur, almond liqueur, coffee liqueur, peppermint schnapps and brandy.

Top coffee with sweetened spicy whipped cream. To make, whip ½ cup whipping cream. Flavor by stirring in 2 tablespoons powdered sugar, ¼ teaspoon ground cinnamon and dash of ground nutmeg.

After Shopping

There are days during the busy holiday season when you can't spare much time for cooking dinner. Shopping, school concerts or holiday preparations call for meals you can make in minutes. Try these main dishes, which you microwave quickly just before serving or prepare the day before for a final, brief reheating.

Fiesta Taco Bake

2 cups uncooked radiatore macaroni
1 lb. ground beef
½ cup chopped onion
1 can (8 oz.) tomato sauce
½ cup mild taco sauce
1 can (4 oz.) chopped green chilies, drained
¼ teaspoon ground cumin
¼ teaspoon salt
1 cup frozen corn
1 cup shredded Cheddar cheese
½ cup shredded mozzarella cheese

4 to 6 servings

Prepare macaroni as directed on package. Rinse and drain. Set aside. In 2-quart casserole, combine ground beef and onion. Microwave at High for 4 to 7 minutes, or until meat is no longer pink, stirring twice. Drain.

Stir in tomato sauce, taco sauce, green chilies, cumin and salt. Spoon about 1 cup of the meat mixture evenly into bottom of 9-inch baking dish. Top with cooked macaroni. Spoon remaining meat mixture over macaroni. Sprinkle evenly with corn. Cover with plastic wrap. ✳ Microwave at High for 7 to 10 minutes, or until center is very hot, rotating dish twice.

Sprinkle cheeses over corn in alternating rows to form 3 Cheddar and 2 mozzarella stripes. Re-cover. Microwave at High for 1 to 2 minutes, or until cheeses melt. Decorate with wedges of tomato and avocado, if desired.

Advance preparation: Up to 24 hours in advance, prepare as directed to ✳ above. Refrigerate. To serve, continue as directed.

Lemony Scallop Salad

¾ lb. fresh spinach, trimmed (about 6 cups)
1 cup plus 2 tablespoons water, divided
1 lb. bay scallops
1 tablespoon cornstarch
1 teaspoon grated lemon peel
2 tablespoons fresh squeezed lemon juice
2 medium carrots, cut into julienne strips (2 × ¼-inch)
2 tablespoons sliced green onion

4 servings

In 3-quart casserole, place spinach and 2 tablespoons water. Cover. Microwave at High for 30 seconds to 1 minute, or until spinach is slightly wilted. Drain. Set aside. Arrange scallops in single layer in 10-inch square casserole. Cover with plastic wrap. Microwave at 70% (Medium High) for 5 to 8 minutes, or until firm and opaque, stirring once. Drain. Set aside.

In 2-quart casserole, combine cornstarch and lemon peel. Blend in remaining 1 cup water and the lemon juice. Stir in carrots. Microwave at High for 6 to 8 minutes, or until sauce is thickened and translucent. Add scallops and onion. Stir to coat. Arrange spinach evenly on 4 serving plates. Before serving, spoon scallop mixture evenly over spinach.

Orange-sauced Flounder Fillets

2 teaspoons cornstarch
⅛ teaspoon ground ginger
    Dash salt
½ cup orange juice
¼ cup dry white wine
¼ cup orange marmalade
1 pkg. (10 oz.) frozen breaded microwave flounder fillets (2 fillets)

2 servings

In 2-cup measure, combine cornstarch, ginger and salt. Blend in remaining ingredients, except fillets. Microwave at High for 2 to 3 minutes, or until mixture is thickened and translucent, stirring once. Cover to keep warm. Set aside.

Microwave fillets as directed on package. Arrange on serving platter. Top with orange sauce.

Vegetable-Ham Combo over Noodles ▲

1 pkg. (10 oz.) uncooked egg noodles
2 tablespoons butter or margarine
¼ cup sliced green onions
¼ cup olive oil
½ teaspoon fennel seeds, crushed
½ teaspoon salt
⅛ teaspoon pepper
2 cups thinly sliced zucchini
1 cup frozen corn
1½ cups julienne fully cooked ham (1½ × ¼-inch strips)
1 large tomato, cut into 16 wedges

4 to 6 servings

Prepare noodles as directed on package. Rinse and drain. Cover. Set aside. In 2-quart casserole, microwave butter at High for 45 seconds to 1 minute, or until melted. Stir in onions, oil, fennel, salt and pepper. Cover. Microwave at High for 1½ to 2 minutes, or until onions are tender.

Stir in zucchini, corn and ham. Re-cover. Microwave at High for 4 to 6½ minutes, or until zucchini is tender, stirring once. Arrange noodles on serving platter. Top with vegetable-ham mixture. Garnish with tomato wedges.

Chicken-Broccoli Pastries

1 pkg. (10 oz.) frozen chopped
  broccoli
1 tablespoon butter or
  margarine
1 tablespoon all-purpose flour
½ teaspoon dried dill weed

½ teaspoon salt
¼ teaspoon dry mustard
⅛ teaspoon garlic powder
  Dash white pepper
¾ cup milk
1 pkg. (3 oz.) cream cheese

1 cup chopped cooked chicken
1 pkg. (8 oz.) refrigerated
  crescent rolls
1 egg white, beaten
  Dill weed

4 servings

Advance preparation: Up to 24 hours in advance, prepare filling to
✱ below. Cover and refrigerate. To serve, continue as directed.

How to Make Chicken-Broccoli Pastries

Place broccoli in 1-quart casserole. Cover. Microwave at High for 4 to 5 minutes, or until defrosted, stirring once to break apart. Drain. Set aside. In 4-cup measure, microwave butter at High for 45 seconds to 1 minute, or until melted.

Stir in flour, ½ teaspoon dill weed, the salt, mustard, garlic powder and pepper. Blend in milk. Microwave at High for 3 to 4 minutes, or until mixture thickens and bubbles, stirring 2 or 3 times.

Place cream cheese in small dish. Microwave at High for 15 to 30 seconds, or until softened. Add to sauce. Beat well with whisk until smooth. Stir in broccoli and chicken.✱ Set aside.

Heat conventional oven to 350°F. Remove crescent roll dough from package. Separate into 4 rectangles. Press perforations to seal. Press or roll each rectangle to 6-inch square.

Spoon about ½ cup of chicken mixture evenly into center of each square. Bring all 4 corners of each square to center. Pinch to seal. Pinch open edges and corners to seal.

Place on ungreased baking sheet. Brush tops of pastries with egg white. Sprinkle lightly with dill weed. Bake for 18 to 24 minutes, or until dark golden brown.

Turkey Stir-fry

¼ cup cornstarch
2 tablespoons sugar
2 teaspoons instant chicken
  bouillon granules
1 teaspoon ground ginger
⅛ teaspoon white pepper
2 cups water
2 tablespoons soy sauce
1 red pepper, cut into 1-inch
  chunks (about 1 cup)
1½ cups cubed cooked turkey
  (¾-inch cubes)
1½ cups sliced bok choy
4 cups fresh bean sprouts

4 servings

In 4-cup measure, combine cornstarch, sugar, bouillon, ginger and pepper. Blend in water and soy sauce. Microwave at High for 5 to 8 minutes, or until sauce is thickened and translucent, stirring every 2 minutes.

In 2-quart casserole, combine sauce and red pepper. Cover. Microwave at High for 2 to 4 minutes, or until red pepper is tender-crisp, stirring once. Add turkey and bok choy. Microwave at High for 3 to 4 minutes, or until hot, stirring once. Serve over bean sprouts.

Easy Cheesy Clam Chowder

1 pkg. (10 oz.) frozen broccoli, cauliflower and carrots in cheese-flavored sauce
2 cans (10¾ oz. each) condensed cream of potato soup
1 can (6½ oz.) minced clams, undrained
½ cup milk
½ cup water
1 tablespoon dried parsley flakes
3 drops red pepper sauce

4 to 6 servings

Advance preparation: Up to 1 day in advance, prepare as directed below. Cover and refrigerate. To serve, microwave at High for 10 to 15 minutes, or until hot, stirring twice.

How to Microwave Easy Cheesy Clam Chowder

Cut a small slit in center of vegetable pouch using scissors. Microwave slit-side-up at High for 4 to 6 minutes, or until defrosted, rotating once. Set aside.

Combine remaining ingredients in 3-quart casserole. Cover. Microwave at High for 6 to 8 minutes, or until mixture is hot, stirring once.

Stir in vegetables and cheese sauce. Mix well. Re-cover. Microwave at High for 5 to 8 minutes, or until chowder is hot, stirring once.

Blizzard of Holiday Ideas

Quick Cookies and Candy Creations

No time for baking? Packaged or bakery cookies give you a head start. Dip them in melted candy coating, then be creative with colored sugars, chopped nuts or multicolored shot. For an afternoon of family fun, enlist the children's help. Create the easy, festive candies from nuts, caramels, microwave-melted chocolate and candy coating.

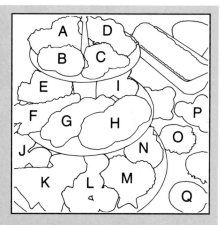

Candy Coating Melting Chart

Amount	Container	Microwave at 50% (Medium)
⅛ lb.*	Small mixing bowl	2-3 min.
¼ lb.	Small mixing bowl	2-4 min.
½ lb.	Small mixing bowl	2½-5 min.
¾ lb.	Medium mixing bowl	2½-5½ min.
1 lb.	Medium mixing bowl	4-8 min.

*⅛ lb. candy coating equals 1 square.

Butter Cookie Wreaths ▲

⅛ lb. white or chocolate-
  flavored candy coating
12 butter cookies (2-inch) with
  hole in center

Red or green colored sugar
Red cinnamon candies
12 pieces shoestring licorice
  (4-inch lengths)

1 dozen cookies

Christmas Jewel Kiss: Follow
recipe left, except omit cinnamon
candies and shoestring licorice.
Place a chocolate kiss in the center of each dipped cookie.

How to Microwave Butter Cookie Wreaths

Line a baking sheet with wax
paper. Set aside. Melt candy
coating as directed in chart,
page 107.

Dip the top of each cookie
into coating. Place cookies
dipped-side-up on prepared
baking sheet.

Decorate each cookie with
colored sugar and cinnamon
candies. Tie licorice into bows,
and use coating to attach to
each cookie. Let stand, or chill,
until set. Store in cool, dry place.

Quick Holiday Cookies ▲

¼ lb. white or chocolate-
    flavored candy coating

12 cookies (2½-inch)
    Multicolored shot

1 dozen cookies

Line a baking sheet with wax paper. Set aside. Melt candy coating as directed in chart, page 107. Dip half of each cookie into coating. Place cookies on prepared baking sheet. Sprinkle dipped portion of each cookie with shot. Let stand, or chill, until set. Store in cool, dry place.

Holiday Nut Crisps

⅛ lb. white or chocolate-
    flavored candy coating
12 vanilla wafer cookies (1½-inch)

⅓ cup chopped walnuts or
    pecans

1 dozen cookies

Line a baking sheet with wax paper. Set aside. Melt candy coating as directed in chart, page 107. Dip half of each cookie into coating. Place cookies on prepared baking sheet. Sprinkle dipped portion of each cookie with chopped nuts. Let stand, or chill, until set. Store in cool, dry place.

Chocolate-dipped Pretzels ▲

⅛ lb. chocolate-flavored candy
    coating
36 small pretzel twists
    Multicolored shot
⅛ lb. white candy coating

3 dozen pretzels

Line a baking sheet with wax paper. Set aside. Melt chocolate-flavored coating as directed in chart, page 107. Dip half of each pretzel into coating. Place pretzels on prepared baking sheet. Sprinkle dipped portion of each pretzel with shot. Let stand, or chill, until set.

Repeat with white coating, dipping undecorated half of each pretzel into coating. Omit shot. Store in cool, dry place.

◄ Wafer Cookie Presents

¼ lb. white candy coating
1 pkg. (10 oz.) cream-filled
   wafer cookies (2½-inch)
   Food color paste*
24 silver balls

2 dozen cookies

Line a baking sheet with wax paper. Set aside. Melt candy coating as directed in chart, page 107. Spoon a small amount of coating onto 24 cookies. Top each cookie with another cookie. Press gently to sandwich together. Place cookies on prepared baking sheet. Set aside.

Tint remaining coating with food color paste. Spoon coating into 1-quart sealable freezer bag. Squeeze coating to one corner of bag. Seal bag. Using scissors, snip corner of bag slightly to form writing tip. Pipe coating across cookie to make ribbon and bow. Place silver ball in center of each bow. Let stand, or chill, until set. Store in cool, dry place.

*Food color paste is available at most food specialty stores. Do not use liquid food coloring.

Appliquéd Holiday Cookies

12 sugar cookies (2½-inch)
4 chewy fruit rolls
   (0.5 oz. each)

1 dozen cookies

Arrange 6 sugar cookies on a plate. Set aside. Unroll 2 fruit rolls. Cut out holiday shapes, using cookie cutter or scissors. Place 1 cutout on each cookie.

Microwave cookies at High for 30 seconds to 1 minute, or just until warm, rotating plate once. (Watch closely to prevent burning.) Pat appliqués gently so they adhere to surface of warm cookies. Repeat with remaining cookies and fruit rolls. Cool completely. Store in cool, dry place.

Fancy Filled Cookies ▶

1 cup ready-to-spread frosting
1 pkg. (5½ oz.) pirouette
    cookies
⅛ lb. white or chocolate-
    flavored candy coating
    Red or green colored sugar
    (optional)
    Multicolored shot (optional)

2 dozen cookies

Line a baking sheet with wax paper. Set aside. Place frosting in 1-quart sealable freezer bag. Squeeze frosting to one corner of bag. Seal bag. Using scissors, snip corner of bag slightly to form tip. Pipe frosting into both ends of each cookie. Place cookies on prepared baking sheet. Set aside.

Melt candy coating as directed in chart, page 107. Spoon coating into another 1-quart sealable freezer bag. Squeeze coating to one corner of bag. Seal bag. Using scissors, snip corner of bag slightly to form writing tip. Pipe coating over filled cookies in zigzag or other decorative pattern. Sprinkle with colored sugar and shot. Let stand, or chill, until set. Store in cool, dry place.

Ginger Man Sandwich Cookies

¼ lb. white candy coating
    Red or green food color
    paste* (optional)
1 pkg. (5 oz.) ginger man
    cookies
10 pieces shoestring licorice
    (4-inch lengths)
    Red cinnamon candies

10 cookies

Line a baking sheet with wax paper. Set aside. Melt candy coating as directed in chart, page 107. Add food color paste. Mix well.

Spoon a small amount of coating onto the back of each of 10 cookies. Place cookies coated-side-up on prepared baking sheet. Fold licorice pieces in half to form loops. Place 1 loop at head end of each cookie, with cut ends in coating on cookie.

Top each cookie with another cookie, right-side-up, and press gently to sandwich together. Decorate one side, using remaining coating to attach cinnamon candies for eyes, nose and buttons. Let stand, or chill, until set. Store in cool, dry place.

*Food color paste is available at most food specialty stores. Do not use liquid food coloring.

Snowman Macaroons ▲

¼ lb. white candy coating
12 macaroon cookies (2-inch)
       Flaked coconut
12 red cinnamon candies
12 raisins, cut in half

12 pieces red shoestring
       licorice (¾-inch lengths)
12 pieces black shoestring
       licorice (½-inch lengths)
¼ cup sugar, divided
24 large black gumdrops

1 dozen cookies

Line a baking sheet with wax paper. Set aside. Melt candy coating as directed in chart, page 107. Dip the top of each cookie into coating. Place cookies dipped-side-up on prepared baking sheet.

Sprinkle each cookie with coconut. Use remaining coating to attach cinnamon candy for nose, raisin halves for eyes and red licorice for mouth. Use black licorice for stem of pipe.

For hat and bowl of pipe, sprinkle 1 teaspoon sugar on piece of wax paper. Place 2 large black gumdrops on sugar. Top with another piece of wax paper. Roll gumdrops between wax paper to ¼-inch thickness. Cut flattened gumdrops into shape of hat and pipe bowl. Attach with coating. Repeat for remaining snowmen. Let stand, or chill, until set. Store in cool, dry place.

◄ Christmas Bear Cookies

¼ lb. white candy coating
12 macaroon cookies (2-inch)
       Flaked coconut
12 red cinnamon candies
12 miniature marshmallows,
       flattened
24 miniature chocolate chips
 6 large marshmallows,
       quartered
       Red colored sugar
12 large gumdrops, cut in half
       lengthwise
12 candy-coated plain
       chocolate pieces

1 dozen cookies

Line a baking sheet with wax paper. Set aside. Melt candy coating as directed in chart, page 107. Dip the top of each cookie into coating. Place cookies dipped-side-up on prepared baking sheet.

Sprinkle each cookie with coconut. To make nose, use remaining coating to attach a cinnamon candy to the center of each flattened marshmallow and to attach nose to each cookie. Attach chocolate chips for eyes. Attach marshmallow quarter to each side of cookie for ears. Spread small amount of coating on each ear, and sprinkle with colored sugar.

Use coating to attach 2 gumdrop halves to make bow tie and to attach candy-coated chocolate piece in center of each bow. Let stand, or chill, until set. Store in cool, dry place.

Santa Cookies ▶

¼ lb. white or chocolate-
    flavored candy coating
12 sugar cookies (2½-inch)
    Red or green colored sugar
    Flaked coconut
6 small gumdrops, cut in half
    crosswise
36 red cinnamon candies

1 dozen cookies

Line a baking sheet with wax paper. Set aside. Melt candy coating as directed in chart, page 107. Dip the top of each cookie into coating. Place cookies dipped-side-up on prepared baking sheet.

Decorate each Santa with red or green colored sugar to make hat, and coconut to make beard. Use gumdrop half to make pom-pom for hat, and cinnamon candies for eyes and nose. Let stand, or chill, until set. Store in cool, dry place.

Santa's Elf Cookies ▼

¼ lb. white candy coating
12 sugar cookies (2½-inch)
    Red or green colored sugar
12 miniature marshmallows

24 chocolate chips
12 red cinnamon candies
12 small red gumdrops, cut in
    half crosswise

12 pieces red shoestring licorice
    (1-inch lengths)

1 dozen cookies

How to Microwave Santa's Elf Cookies

Line a baking sheet with wax paper. Set aside. Melt candy coating as directed in chart, page 107. Dip half of each cookie into coating to make hat.

Place cookies on prepared baking sheet. Sprinkle hat with colored sugar. Use remaining coating to attach marshmallow for pom-pom of hat, and chocolate chips for eyes.

Attach cinnamon candy for nose, gumdrop halves for cheeks and piece of licorice for mouth. Let stand, or chill, until set. Store in cool, dry place.

◄ Chocolate Cherry Cups

20 small paper candy cups
 1 cup chocolate chips or 1
     (6 oz.) white baking bar,
     broken into pieces

20 red or green candied
     cherries

20 candies

Place candy cups on a baking sheet. Set aside. Place chocolate chips in small mixing bowl. Microwave at 50% (Medium) for 3½ to 4½ minutes, or until chocolate is glossy and can be stirred smooth, stirring once or twice.

Spoon chocolate evenly into candy cups, filling three-fourths full. Top each candy with candied cherry. Let stand, or chill, until set. Cover and store in refrigerator.

◄ Crunchy Caramel Chews

20 small paper candy cups
10 caramels, cut into quarters

 1 cup chocolate chips or 1
     (6 oz.) white baking bar,
     broken into pieces
¼   cup crisp rice cereal

20 candies

Place candy cups on a baking sheet. Place 2 pieces of caramel in each candy cup. Set aside. Place chocolate chips in small mixing bowl. Microwave at 50% (Medium) for 3½ to 4½ minutes, or until chocolate is glossy and can be stirred smooth, stirring once or twice.

Spoon chocolate evenly over caramels, filling candy cups. Sprinkle each candy with cereal. Let stand, or chill, until set. Cover and store in refrigerator.

◄ Raisin-Pecan Clusters

20 small paper candy cups
⅓   cup raisins, divided
40 pecan halves, divided

 1 cup chocolate chips or 1
     (6 oz.) white baking bar,
     broken into pieces

20 candies

Place candy cups on a baking sheet. In each candy cup, place about 6 raisins and 1 pecan half. Set aside. Place chocolate chips in small mixing bowl. Microwave at 50% (Medium) for 3½ to 4½ minutes, or until chocolate is glossy and can be stirred smooth, stirring once or twice.

Spoon chocolate evenly over raisins and pecan halves, filling candy cups full. Top each candy with 1 pecan half. Let stand, or chill, until set. Cover and store in refrigerator.

Peanut Clusters: Follow recipe above, except in each candy cup substitute 4 dry-roasted peanuts for raisins and pecan half. Substitute 4 peanut halves for pecan half on top of each candy.

Macadamia Nut Clusters: Follow recipe above, except in each candy cup substitute 3 macadamia nuts for raisins and pecan half. Substitute 1 macadamia nut for pecan half on top of each candy.

Jordan Almond Bark

1¼ lbs. white candy coating
½ lb. Jordan almonds
½ cup unblanched whole
    almonds

2 lbs.

Jelly Bean Bark: Follow recipe above, except substitute 2 cups jelly beans for almonds.

How to Microwave Jordan Almond Bark

Line a baking sheet with foil. Set aside. In 2-quart casserole, microwave candy coating at 50% (Medium) for 4 to 6 minutes, or until coating can be stirred smooth, stirring twice. Stir in almonds.

Spread to ¼ to ½-inch thickness on prepared baking sheet. Let stand, or chill, until set. Break into pieces. Store in cool, dry place.

Chocolate Holiday Cutouts ▶

3 pkgs. (4 oz. each) German
    sweet chocolate, broken up
2 pkgs. (6 oz. each) white
    baking bar, broken up
    Colored sugar

                1½ lbs.

Mint Chocolate Cutouts: Follow recipe left, except substitute 12 oz. semisweet mint chocolate chips for German sweet chocolate.

Crispy Cutouts: Follow recipe left, except sprinkle 1 cup crisp rice cereal evenly over rectangle of melted German sweet chocolate, and omit colored sugar.

Chocolate-Nut Cutouts: Follow recipe left, except sprinkle 1 cup chopped pecans evenly over rectangle of melted German sweet chocolate, and omit colored sugar.

How to Make Chocolate Holiday Cutouts

Use pencil to trace 14 × 9-inch rectangle on wax paper. Place wax paper in 15½ × 10½-inch jelly roll pan. Set aside.

Place chocolate pieces in 8-cup measure. Microwave at 50% (Medium) for 3 to 5 minutes, or until chocolate is glossy and can be stirred smooth, stirring twice.

Pour and spread chocolate evenly within 14 × 9-inch rectangle on prepared jelly roll pan. Place in freezer 5 minutes, or until set.

Place baking bar pieces in 8-cup measure. Microwave at 50% (Medium) for 3 to 5 minutes, or until mixture is glossy and can be stirred smooth, stirring twice. Cool slightly. Pour and spread evenly over chocolate layer.

Sprinkle baking bar layer with colored sugar. Place in freezer 5 minutes, or until set. Remove from freezer. Let stand about 10 minutes, or until slightly thawed.

Cut desired shapes, using metal cookie cutters or sharp knife. Place on plate in single layer. Cover with plastic wrap. Chill until set.

Chocolate Place Cards or Gift Tags ▲

1 recipe Chocolate Holiday
  Cutouts (opposite)
⅛ lb. chocolate-flavored candy
  coating

  42 cards or tags

Prepare Chocolate Holiday Cutouts as directed. Use sharp knife to cut 3 × 1-inch rectangles or cut into shapes with cookie cutters. For Gift Tags, cut hole in one end with tip of sharp knife. Melt candy coating as directed in chart, page 107. Spoon coating into 1-quart sealable freezer bag. Squeeze coating to one corner of bag. Seal bag. Using scissors, snip corner of bag slightly to form writing tip.

Pipe names over sugar sprinkles. Let stand, or chill, until set. Wrap each card or tag in small piece of plastic wrap. Use place cards for holiday table setting. Tie gift tags with ribbon and attach to presents.

Lacy Chocolate Basket

⅛ lb. chocolate-flavored candy
    coating
¼ lb. white candy coating,
    divided

1 basket

Decorations

*For centuries, decorating with food expressed the spirit
of holiday bounty. The microwave oven helps you continue this
tradition in contemporary style. Create edible decorations to
deck your own halls or to give as gifts.*

How to Make Lacy Chocolate Basket

Invert a small shallow dish (about 5-inch). Cover with foil. Smooth foil down tightly to remove large wrinkles. Place foil-covered dish in freezer for at least 30 minutes, or overnight.

Place chocolate-flavored candy coating in small bowl. Microwave at 50% (Medium) for 2 to 3 minutes, or until coating can be stirred smooth. Spoon into 1-quart sealable freezer bag. Squeeze to one corner of bag. Seal bag.

Use scissors to snip corner of bag slightly to form writing tip. Remove foil-wrapped dish from freezer. Pipe melted coating over dish in looping, lacy pattern. Return dish to freezer for 10 minutes.

Place ⅛ lb. white candy coating in small bowl. Microwave at 50% (Medium) for 2 to 3 minutes, or until coating can be stirred smooth. Spoon into another 1-quart sealable freezer bag. Squeeze to one corner of bag. Seal bag.

Use scissors to snip corner of bag slightly to form writing tip. Pipe coating over first layer in looping, lacy pattern. Freeze for 10 minutes. Repeat with remaining ⅛ lb. white candy coating.

Remove dish and then foil carefully from inside of candy basket. Fill basket with jelly beans, gumdrops or cookies. Baskets are fragile, so handle carefully. Store in cool, dry place away from direct heat.

119

Candy Treasure Chest

1 lb. white candy coating
¼ lb. chocolate-flavored candy
   coating

Red or green colored sugar
  (optional)

1 chest

How to Make Candy Treasure Chest

Line a 15½ × 10½-inch jelly roll pan with wax paper. Set aside. In 8-cup measure, microwave white candy coating at 50% (Medium) for 3 to 5 minutes, or until coating can be stirred smooth, stirring once or twice.

Pour and spread coating evenly into prepared pan to within ½ inch of edges. Place in freezer for 10 minutes, or until coating is set. Let stand at room temperature for 30 minutes before cutting.

Cut 6 rectangles: two 5 × 6-inch (bottom and top), two 5 × 2-inch (short sides), two 6 × 2-inch (long sides), using 8-inch chef's knife. Place scraps in 2-cup measure. Microwave at 50% (Medium) for 1 to 2 minutes, or until coating can be stirred smooth.

Spoon coating into 1-quart sealable freezer bag. Squeeze to one corner of bag. Seal bag. Using scissors, snip corner of bag slightly to form writing tip. Place one 5 × 6-inch rectangle on wax paper. Pipe coating along edges. Place sides of chest upright along edges of bottom, piping additional coating between edges to secure sides.

Place chocolate coating in 2-cup measure. Microwave at 50% (Medium) for 2 to 4 minutes, or until coating can be stirred smooth. Spoon into another 1-quart sealable freezer bag. Squeeze to one corner of bag. Seal bag. Using scissors, snip corner of bag slightly to form writing tip. Pipe coating along top edges of chest. Before set, sprinkle edges with colored sugar.

Make lid for chest by piping coating around edges of remaining rectangle. Pipe holiday messages or designs on top. Let stand, or chill, until set. Fill chest with candy. Top with lid. Chests are fragile, so handle carefully. Store in cool, dry place away from direct heat.

Decorated Cone Trees

Line a baking sheet with wax paper. Set aside. In 8-cup measure, microwave 1 lb. white or chocolate-flavored candy coating at 50% (Medium) for 4 to 6 minutes, or until coating can be stirred smooth.

Stand 8 sugar cones on prepared baking sheet. Spoon coating over cones, covering outside. Decorate as directed below. Let stand, or chill, until coating is set.

Popcorn and Red Cinnamon Candy Tree:
Attach pieces of popped popcorn and red cinnamon candies by pressing lightly into candy coating. Top with popped kernel of corn.

Gumdrop Tree: Attach small colored gumdrop halves randomly over coated tree cone. Top tree with star cut from flattened gumdrop.

Silver Ball Tree: Sprinkle silver balls over coated tree cone. Top tree with shoestring licorice bow or with star cut from flattened gumdrop.

Drizzled Snow-capped Tree: Coat cones as directed left. Let stand, or chill, until coating is set. Place ¼ lb. candy coating of a contrasting color in 1-cup measure. Microwave at High for 3 to 4 minutes, or until coating can be stirred smooth. Drizzle contrasting coating over each coated tree. Sprinkle with red or green colored sugar.

Frosted Fruity Wreaths

¾ lb. white candy coating,
    divided
5 cups frosted fruit-flavored
    corn puff cereal
    Red or green colored sugar
    (optional)
12 large gumdrops, cut in half
    lengthwise
12 candy-coated plain
    chocolate pieces

1 dozen wreaths

Line 2 baking sheets with wax paper. Set aside. Place ½ lb. coating in large mixing bowl. Microwave at 50% (Medium) for 2½ to 5 minutes, or until coating can be stirred smooth. Add cereal. Stir to coat. Spoon about one-twelfth of mixture onto prepared baking sheet. Shape into 3-inch wreath. Sprinkle with colored sugar. Repeat with remaining mixture, placing 6 wreaths on each prepared baking sheet.

Place remaining ¼ lb. coating in small mixing bowl. Microwave at 50% (Medium) for 2 to 4 minutes, or until melted, stirring once. Spoon into sealable freezer bag. Squeeze coating to one corner of bag. Seal bag. Using scissors, snip corner of bag slightly to form writing tip. Drizzle all but small amount of coating over wreaths. Use remaining coating to attach 2 gumdrop halves for bow at base of each wreath. At-tach 1 candy-coated chocolate piece in center of each bow. Let wreaths stand, or chill, until set. Hang in cool, dry place.

Chow Mein Wreath Cookies:
Follow recipe above, except sub-stitute ½ lb. chocolate-flavored candy coating for ½ lb. white candy coating, and 5 cups chow mein noodles for fruit-flavored corn puff cereal. Omit large gum-drops and candy-coated plain chocolate pieces. Decorate with red cinnamon candies for holly berries, and gumdrop leaves, sliced lengthwise, for holly leaves.

Reindeer Centerpiece ◀

1 lb. white candy coating, divided
20 homemade gingerbread reindeer cookies (about 2½-inch)
10 vanilla wafer cookies
1 cup flaked coconut
2 pieces (each 38 inches long) red shoestring licorice
1 red cinnamon candy

Out of heavy cardboard, cut an elongated S-shape base measuring about 24 inches long and 2½ inches wide. Cover base with foil. Set aside.

Line a baking sheet with wax paper. Melt ¼ lb. candy coating as directed in chart, page 107. Spoon a small amount of melted coating onto the back of each of 10 cookies. Place coated-side-up on prepared baking sheet. Top each of these cookies with another and press gently to sandwich. Let stand or chill until set.

Use the remaining melted coating to attach each reindeer sandwich to a vanilla wafer cookie. Attach 5 reindeer front-hooves-down, and 5, hind-hooves-down. Hold each reindeer sandwich upright on wafer cookie until coating is set. (This allows reindeer to stand upright.)

In a medium mixing bowl, melt remaining ¾ lb. coating as directed in chart, page 107. Spoon evenly over foil-covered base. Stand reindeer cookies end to end on base. Sprinkle base with coconut. Let stand until set.

Tie shoestring licorice pieces together in a bow. Tuck under chin of lead reindeer and continue crisscrossing licorice between reindeer. Tie at end to secure. Use coating to attach red cinnamon candy to tip of nose of lead reindeer.

Gumdrop Candle Wreath ▲

½ lb. white candy coating
2 pkgs. (10¾ oz. each) large gumdrops, divided

6 spearmint gumdrop leaves, cut in half lengthwise

1 wreath

Line the base of a 10-inch removable-bottom angel food cake pan with foil. In small mixing bowl, microwave candy coating at 50% (Medium) for 2½ to 5 minutes, or until coating can be stirred smooth. Reserve 1 tablespoon melted coating in small bowl. Set aside.

Pour remaining melted candy coating evenly into bottom of prepared cake pan. Reserve 3 gumdrops. Stand remaining gumdrops upright in melted coating, alternating colors. Let stand, or chill, until set. Remove gumdrop wreath from pan. Remove foil. Slice reserved gumdrops in half crosswise.

If necessary, microwave reserved candy coating at 50% (Medium) for 30 to 45 seconds, or until coating can be stirred smooth. Use coating to attach 1 gumdrop slice and 2 leaf slices on wreath. Continue attaching remaining gumdrop and leaf slices. Let wreath stand, or chill, until set. Place 2-inch candle in center and use as holiday centerpiece. Set in cool, dry place away from direct heat.

Pretzel Candy Cane

 1 lb. white candy coating,
     divided
20 large pretzel twists
     Red food color paste*
     Green food color paste*

1 candy cane

Line a baking sheet with wax paper. Set aside. In medium mixing bowl, microwave ¾ lb. candy coating at 50% (Medium) for 2½ to 5½ minutes, or until coating can be stirred smooth. Dip 7 pretzels, one at a time, in coating. On prepared baking sheet, arrange pretzels end to end in candy cane shape.

Dip 6 more pretzels, one at a time, in coating. Arrange dipped pretzels over first layer of pretzels at points where 2 pretzels meet. Dip remaining pretzels, one at a time, in coating, and arrange over second layer.

In small bowl, microwave ⅛ lb. coating at 50% (Medium) for 2 to 3 minutes, or until coating can be stirred smooth. Tint lightly with red food color paste. Spoon into 1-quart sealable freezer bag. Squeeze to one corner of bag. Seal bag. Using scissors, snip corner of bag slightly to form writing tip. Drizzle coating across candy cane. Repeat with remaining ⅛ lb. coating and the green food color paste. Let stand, or chill, until set. Tie with bow. Set in cool, dry place away from direct heat and sunlight.

*Food color paste is available at most food specialty stores. Do not use liquid food coloring.

Glazed Nut Wreath

6 cups mixed nuts in the shell
   (about 1¾ lbs.)
2 tablespoons shortening,
   divided

2 cups sugar
1 cup corn syrup
½ cup water

1 wreath

NOTE: Placing nuts in mold requires 2 people and must be done very quickly before the syrup sets. Recipe not recommended for ovens with less than 600 cooking watts.

How to Microwave Glazed Nut Wreath

Place nuts in large mixing bowl. Set aside. Line a 6½-cup ring mold with foil. Grease foil with 1 tablespoon shortening. Set aside. Grease a 14-inch sheet of foil with remaining 1 tablespoon shortening. Set aside.

Combine remaining ingredients in 8-cup measure. Insert microwave candy thermometer. Microwave at High for 15 to 20 minutes, or until thermometer registers 310°F (hard crack stage, page 130).

Remove thermometer. Immediately pour syrup over nuts in bowl, tossing quickly to coat. Spoon evenly into prepared ring mold. With buttered fingers, press lightly to pack nuts into mold. Cool 10 minutes.

Unmold nut mixture carefully onto prepared sheet of foil. Press into desired wreath shape. Let stand 24 hours before decorating. Attach bow with wire, if desired. Use as centerpiece, or hang in cool, dry place away from direct heat and sunlight.

Microwave Gift Ideas

Nothing speaks of caring friendship more personally than a gift from your kitchen. This section includes private-label preserves, distinctive candies and flavored nuts, and fragrant potpourri to scent the winter air. Package your present in a pretty or practical container, such as a champagne glass, a mug, a decorative jar or a basket.

Carrot Relish

2 cups chopped carrots
1 cup chopped cucumber, peeled and seeded
¾ cup chopped celery
¾ cup sugar
¾ cup white vinegar
½ cup chopped green pepper
½ cup chopped onion
2 teaspoons pickling salt
2 teaspoons mustard seed
½ teaspoon ground ginger
¼ teaspoon red pepper sauce
⅛ teaspoon ground cloves

Three ½-pint jars

In 2-quart casserole, place all ingredients. Mix well. Cover. Microwave at High for 15 minutes, stirring once or twice. Microwave, uncovered, at High for 20 to 25 minutes longer, or until mixture thickens slightly, stirring twice.

Spoon relish into 3 sterilized ½-pint jars. Cover and refrigerate for no longer than 1 month. Serve as a condiment with pork roast, ham, sausages and wieners.

For gift giving, decorate jar lids with cloth covers and ribbons. Include decorative labels that list contents, serving and storage instructions.

Curried Pear Chutney

1 cup packed brown sugar
¼ cup cider vinegar
1½ teaspoons curry powder
½ teaspoon salt
½ teaspoon ground cinnamon
2 large pears, chopped (about 3 cups)
1 large orange, peeled and chopped (about 1 cup)
½ cup chopped green pepper
½ cup chopped red pepper
½ cup golden raisins
½ cup slivered almonds

Two ½-pint jars

In 2-quart casserole, combine brown sugar, vinegar, curry powder, salt and cinnamon. Microwave at High for 1½ to 3 minutes, or until sugar dissolves, stirring once. Stir in remaining ingredients, except almonds. Microwave at High for 30 to 50 minutes, or until liquid is syrupy and fruit is very tender, stirring 2 or 3 times. Stir in almonds. Cool slightly.

Spoon chutney into 2 sterilized ½-pint jars. Cover and refrigerate no longer than 2 weeks. Serve as a condiment with lamb, pork or chicken.

For gift giving, decorate jar lids with cloth covers and ribbons. Include decorative labels that list contents, serving and storage instructions.

Pink Champagne Jelly

2¾ cups pink champagne
1 pkg. (3 oz.) liquid fruit pectin
½ teaspoon ground cardamom
¼ teaspoon ground allspice
3½ cups sugar
Paraffin wax

Nine 4-oz. glasses

In 8-cup measure, combine all ingredients, except sugar and paraffin. Microwave at High for 8 to 12 minutes, or until boiling, stirring after every 4 minutes. Boil 1 minute. Gradually stir in sugar until blended.

Microwave at High for 3 to 6 minutes, or until mixture returns to a boil, stirring every 2 minutes to prevent boil-over. Boil 1 minute. Skim any foam from top.

Pour jelly evenly into each of 9 sterilized, straight-sided 4-oz. champagne glasses to within ½ inch from top.

Melt paraffin conventionally in small saucepan over medium heat. (Paraffin is transparent to microwave energy and cannot be melted in the microwave.) While jelly is hot, cover with ⅛ inch of paraffin. When jelly is cool, add another ⅛ inch of paraffin for final sealing. Refrigerate jelly no longer than 1 month.

Make decorative labels for gift giving by tracing a cookie cutter on heavy paper, such as plain note cards. Use colored markers to decorate labels. Include instructions for storage. Place on paraffin just after final sealing.

Cashew Toffee ▲

1 cup plus 1 tablespoon
  butter or margarine,
  divided
1¼ cups chopped cashews,
  divided
2 cups sugar
2 tablespoons light corn syrup

2 tablespoons water
⅛ teaspoon cream of tartar
1 teaspoon vanilla
1 pkg. (12 oz.) vanilla milk
  chips or semisweet
  chocolate chips

2½ lbs.

Line a 15½ × 10½-inch jelly roll pan with foil. Grease foil with 1 table-spoon butter. Sprinkle 1 cup cashews in an even layer in prepared pan. Set aside.

In an 8-cup measure, microwave remaining 1 cup butter at High for 1½ to 2 minutes, or until melted. Stir in sugar, corn syrup, water and cream of tartar. Microwave at High for 4 minutes. Mix well. Insert microwave candy thermometer. Microwave mixture at High for 5½ to 7½ minutes, or until thermometer registers 290°F (soft crack stage, right). Remove thermometer.

Stir in vanilla. Pour slowly and evenly over nuts in pan. Immediately sprinkle with vanilla chips. Let stand about 1 minute. Spread chips over toffee mixture. Sprinkle with remaining ¼ cup cashews. Cool completely. Break into pieces. Store in airtight container.

For gift giving, place toffee in clear glass candy dish, or arrange on glass plate. Cover with plastic wrap. Decorate with ribbons. Include a decorative label that lists contents.

NOTE: Recipe not recommended for ovens with less than 600 cooking watts.

How to Test Candy for Doneness

If you don't have a microwave-safe candy thermometer, use cold water test to judge done-ness. Fill a cup with very cold water. Drop about ½ teaspoon of mixture into the cup, and let stand for a few seconds. Then test syrup with your fingers.

Soft Crack Stage: Syrup separates into hard *but not* brittle threads (pictured).

Hard Crack Stage: Syrup separates into hard *and* brittle threads.

◄ Filbert Brittle

2 tablespoons butter or margarine, divided
½ cup granulated sugar
½ cup packed brown sugar
½ cup light corn syrup
⅛ teaspoon salt
¾ cup chopped filberts
2 teaspoons lemon extract
1 teaspoon baking soda

1 lb.

Line a baking sheet with foil. Grease foil with 1 tablespoon butter. Set aside. In 8-cup measure, combine sugars, corn syrup and salt. Mix well. Microwave at High for 5 minutes. Stir in filberts.

Insert microwave candy thermometer. Microwave at High for 3½ to 6 minutes, or until thermometer registers 300°F (hard crack stage, left), stirring every 2 minutes. Remove thermometer. Quickly stir in remaining 1 tablespoon butter, the lemon extract and baking soda until mixture is light and foamy.

Spread to ¼-inch thickness on prepared baking sheet. Cool completely. Break into pieces. Store in airtight container.

For gift giving, arrange brittle in a brandy snifter or clear glass canister. Cover with plastic wrap. Decorate with ribbons. Include a decorative label that lists contents.

Peanut Brittle: Follow recipe above, except substitute 1 cup shelled raw peanuts for filberts, and 1½ teaspoons vanilla for lemon extract. Microwave as directed above. After stirring in peanuts, microwave at High for 5 to 10 minutes, or until thermometer registers 300°F, stirring every 2 minutes. Continue as directed.

Mint Swirl Fudge ▲

1 tablespoon shortening
1 pkg. (3 oz.) cream cheese
1 can (14 oz.) sweetened condensed milk, divided
¼ teaspoon mint extract
1 to 2 drops green food coloring

3 pkg. (6 oz. each) semisweet chocolate chips
1 tablespoon butter or margarine
½ teaspoon vanilla
Green colored sugar

2¼ lbs.

Line a 9-inch pie plate with foil. Grease with shortening. Set aside. In medium mixing bowl, microwave cream cheese at High for 15 to 30 seconds, or until softened. Add 2 tablespoons milk, the mint extract and food coloring. Beat at low speed of electric mixer until smooth. Set aside.

In an 8-cup measure, combine remaining milk, the chocolate chips and butter. Microwave at 50% (Medium) for 2 to 3½ minutes, or until mixture is glossy and can be stirred smooth, stirring twice. Stir in vanilla.

Pour into prepared pie plate. Smooth with spatula. Drop cream cheese mixture by spoonfuls over chocolate mixture. Use spatula to swirl decoratively into chocolate. Sprinkle with sugar. Chill until firm. Cut into squares. Store in cool, dry place.

For gift giving, leave fudge in pie plate. Cover with plastic wrap. Decorate with ribbons. Include a decorative label that lists contents and storage instructions.

Raspberry Tea Mix

Tea Mix:

1¼ cups sugar
 1 cup instant unsweetened
   tea
 2 pkgs. (0.17 oz. each)
   raspberry-flavored
   unsweetened soft drink mix

For one serving:
 1 cup hot water
 2 to 3 tablespoons tea mix

16 servings

Strawberry Tea Mix: Follow recipe above, except substitute strawberry-flavored unsweetened soft drink mix for raspberry-flavored unsweetened soft drink mix.

How to Microwave Raspberry Tea Mix

Combine all tea mix ingredients in medium mixing bowl. Store in airtight container no longer than 6 months.

Place hot water in large mug for 1 serving. Microwave at High for 1 to 2 minutes, or until very hot. Stir in tea mix.

How to Gift Wrap Raspberry Tea Mix

Line 8 to 12-oz. mugs with small plastic food-storage bags for gift giving. Fill each bag with tea mix. Tie ribbon at top of bag to close.

Decorate handle of mug with bow, and attach old-fashioned candy sticks for stirrers. Include decorative label that lists contents, serving and storage instructions.

Carnival Drink Mix ▶

Drink Mix:

2½ cups instant nonfat dry milk powder

2 cups multicolored miniature marshmallows

1 cup strawberry-flavored mix for milk

½ cup powdered sugar

⅓ cup buttermilk powder

⅓ cup powdered nondairy creamer

For one serving:

¾ cup hot water

⅓ cup drink mix

16 servings

In medium mixing bowl, combine all drink mix ingredients. Mix well. Store in airtight container no longer than 6 months.

For 1 serving, place hot water in large mug. Microwave at High for 1 to 2 minutes, or until very hot. Stir in drink mix.

For gift giving, place drink mix in clear glass canisters. Decorate canisters with ribbons. Include decorative label that lists contents, serving and storage instructions.

Hot Chocolate Malted: Follow recipe above, except substitute plain miniature marshmallows for multicolored marshmallows, chocolate-flavored mix for strawberry-flavored mix, and instant malted milk powder for buttermilk powder.

Cinnamon Cocoa Coffee

Coffee Mix:

2 cups sugar

1½ cups instant coffee crystals

1 cup powdered nondairy creamer

½ cup cocoa

½ teaspoon ground cinnamon

For one serving:

1 cup hot water

2 to 3 tablespoons coffee mix

40 servings

In medium mixing bowl, combine all coffee mix ingredients. Store in airtight container no longer than 6 months.

For 1 serving, place hot water in large mug. Microwave at High for 1 to 2 minutes, or until very hot. Stir in coffee mix.

For gift giving, place coffee mix in clear glass canisters. Decorate canisters with ribbons. Include decorative label that lists contents, serving and storage instructions.

How to Microwave Elegant Raspberry Sauce

Elegant Raspberry Sauce

2 pkgs. (12 oz. each) frozen red
   raspberries
1 large orange
1 cup sugar
¾ cup light corn syrup
4 tablespoons black raspberry
   liqueur

Two 1-pint jars

Microwave raspberries in 8-cup measure at High for 5 to 8 minutes, or until defrosted, stirring gently once. Set aside.

Cut long strips (or zest) from orange, using sharp knife and being careful not to remove white membrane with peel. Cut strips into 1-inch lengths. Reserve orange for future use.

Place orange peel, sugar and corn syrup in 4-cup measure. Mix well. Microwave at High for 4 to 5 minutes, or just until sugar mixture boils, stirring once.

Add sugar mixture and liqueur to berries. Stir gently until combined. Pour into 2 sterilized 1-pint jars. Cover and refrigerate no longer than 1 month. Serve over fresh fruit, ice cream or pound cake.

Decorate jar lids with cloth covers and ribbons for gift giving. Include decorative labels that list contents, serving and storage instructions.

134

Rum-Butterscotch Sauce ▲

1½ cups packed brown sugar
½ cup butter or margarine
¼ cup dark corn syrup
1½ cups half-and-half
2 teaspoons imitation rum
  extract

Three ½-pint jars

In 2-quart casserole, combine brown sugar, butter and corn syrup. Microwave at High for 3 to 6 minutes, or until brown sugar dissolves and mixture boils, stirring after every minute. Blend in remaining ingredients.

Pour sauce into 3 sterilized ½-pint jars. Cover and refrigerate no longer than 1 month. To reheat 1 cup of sauce, remove lid from jar. Microwave at High for 1 to 1½ minutes, or until mixture is warm and can be stirred smooth, stirring every 30 seconds. Serve over ice cream or pound cake.

For gift giving, decorate jar lids with cloth covers and ribbons. Include decorative labels that list contents, serving, heating and storage instructions.

Mint Chocolate Sauce ▲

1 cup semisweet chocolate
  chips
¼ cup butter or margarine
2 tablespoons light corn syrup
1 cup whipping cream
½ cup finely crushed
  peppermint candy

Two ½-pint jars

In 2-quart casserole, combine chocolate chips, butter and corn syrup. Microwave at 50% (Medium) for 4 to 5 minutes, or until mixture melts, stirring 2 or 3 times. Blend in whipping cream, using whisk. Microwave at High for 1 minute. Stir in candy.

Pour into 2 sterilized ½-pint jars. Cover and refrigerate no longer than 1 month. To reheat 1 cup of sauce, remove lid from jar. Microwave at High for 1 to 1½ minutes, or until mixture is warm and can be stirred smooth, stirring every 30 seconds. Serve over ice cream or cheesecake.

For gift giving, decorate jar lids with cloth covers and ribbons. Include decorative labels that list contents, serving, heating and storage instructions.

Ginger Oriental Sauce

½ cup finely chopped green
  pepper
2 teaspoons grated fresh
  gingerroot
2 tablespoons vegetable oil
1 cup apricot preserves
1 cup catsup
⅓ cup vinegar
2 tablespoons soy sauce
2 teaspoons sesame oil

Three ½-pint jars

In 2-quart casserole, combine green pepper, gingerroot and vegetable oil. Microwave at High for 2 to 3½ minutes, or until pepper is tender, stirring once. Stir in remaining ingredients. Microwave at High for 9 to 12 minutes, or until sauce begins to thicken, stirring twice.

Pour sauce into 3 sterilized ½-pint jars. Cover and refrigerate no longer than 1 month. Serve with ribs, chicken or fish.

For gift giving, decorate jar lids with cloth covers and ribbons. Include decorative labels that list contents, serving, and storage instructions.

Sherried Mixed Nuts ▲

¼ cup dry sherry
2 tablespoons light corn syrup
¼ teaspoon ground allspice
1 can (12 oz.) salted mixed nuts

¾ lb.

Line a baking sheet with foil. Set aside. In medium mixing bowl, combine all ingredients, except nuts. Mix well. Add nuts. Toss to coat. Spoon evenly into 10-inch pie plate. Microwave at High for 6½ to 8½ minutes, or until liquid is absorbed and nuts are glazed, stirring every 2 minutes.

Spread nuts on prepared baking sheet. Cool completely. Cover and store in cool, dry place no longer than 2 weeks.

For gift giving, place nuts in clear glass canister or nut dish. Cover nut dish with plastic wrap. Decorate with ribbons. Include decorative label that lists contents and storage instructions.

Rosemary-flavored Walnuts ▲

1 tablespoon butter or margarine
2 teaspoons Worcestershire sauce
¾ teaspoon dried rosemary leaves, crushed
½ teaspoon lemon pepper seasoning
1 pkg. (8 oz.) walnut halves

½ lb.

Line a baking sheet with paper towels. In 9-inch pie plate, microwave butter at High for 45 seconds to 1 minute, or until melted. Add remaining ingredients, except walnuts. Mix well.

Add walnuts, stirring to coat. Microwave at High for 4 to 6 minutes, or until butter is absorbed, stirring every 2 minutes. Spread on prepared baking sheet to cool. Cover and store in cool, dry place no longer than 2 weeks.

For gift giving, place nuts in clear glass canister or nut dish. Cover nut dish with plastic wrap. Decorate with ribbons. Include decorative label that lists contents and storage instructions.

◄ Holiday Cheese Spread

Cheese Spread:
- 4 slices bacon
- ½ cup butter or margarine, cut into 1-inch cubes
- 1 pkg. (3 oz.) cream cheese, cut into 1-inch cubes
- 2 cups finely shredded Cheddar cheese
- 2 cups finely shredded Swiss cheese
- 1 teaspoon caraway seed
- ½ teaspoon onion powder
- ⅛ teaspoon garlic powder

Snowman:
- 2 pretzel sticks
- 3 capers
- 3 black peppercorns
- 1 whole pimiento
- 1 pimiento-stuffed green olive
- 1 round buttery cracker

Santa's Boot:
- Sliced almonds
- 5 black peppercorns
- Pimiento strips

2 cheese spreads
(about ¾ lb. each)

How to Make Holiday Cheese Spread

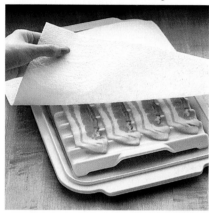

Place bacon on roasting rack. Cover with paper towel. Microwave at High for 3 to 6 minutes, or until brown and crisp. Cool slightly. Crumble and set aside.

Combine butter and cream cheese in medium mixing bowl. Microwave at 30% (Medium Low) for 1½ to 2½ minutes, or until softened, stirring once. Stir in remaining cheese spread ingredients. Mix well. Divide mixture in half.

Make snowman by dividing one-half of cheese mixture into 3 portions. Shape each portion into ball, making balls for head and upper body slightly smaller than base. Stack balls on serving tray.

Make snowman's arms by inserting pretzel sticks into cheese. Use capers for buttons, and peppercorns for eyes and nose. Cut small piece of pimiento for mouth.

Cut ½-inch-wide strip of pimiento to make scarf. Trim top and bottom from olive, and use wooden pick to secure olive to cracker for hat. Place on snowman's head. Cover and refrigerate no longer than 1 week.

Make Santa's boot by forming remaining half of cheese mixture into boot shape. Trim top of boot with sliced almonds for fur. Use peppercorns and pimiento for laces and bow. Cover and refrigerate no longer than 1 week.

Citrus-Spice Potpourri ▲

1 orange
1 lemon
1 lime
⅓ cup water
¼ cup whole cloves
2 tablespoons whole allspice
3 cinnamon sticks, broken up
4 bay leaves, crumbled

1 cup

How to Microwave Citrus-Spice Potpourri

Cut long strips (or zest) from orange, lemon and lime, using sharp knife and being careful not to remove white membrane with peel. Cut strips into 1-inch lengths. Reserve fruit for future use.

Place peels in single layer on paper-towel-lined plate. Pour water into 1-cup measure. Place water next to plate in microwave oven. Microwave at High for 4 to 5 minutes, or just until peels begin to dry, tossing with fingers after every minute.

◄ Woods-scent Potpourri

½ cup fresh pine needles
¼ cup juniper berries
2 tablespoons dried rosemary leaves
1 tablespoon celery seed
1 tablespoon caraway seed
6 bay leaves, crumbled

1 cup

In small plastic food-storage bag, combine all ingredients. Secure bag. Shake to mix.

For gift giving, place dry potpourri in small plastic food-storage bag. Tie ribbon at top of bag to close. Place in small bowl with handle. Include decorative label that lists contents and instructions for use.

To scent room, place 1 cup hot water and 1 tablespoon potpourri in small bowl with handle. Microwave at High for 2 to 3 minutes, or until boiling. Remove from oven. Let potpourri stand. When cool, microwave as directed once or twice more.

Remove peels to another paper towel. Air dry for 24 hours. Place dried peels in small plastic food-storage bag. Add remaining potpourri ingredients. Secure bag. Shake to mix.

Place dry potpourri in small plastic food-storage bag for gift giving. Tie ribbon at top of bag to close. Place in small bowl with handle. Include decorative label that lists contents and instructions for use.

Scent room by placing 1 cup hot water and 1 tablespoon dry potpourri in small bowl with handle. Microwave at High for 2 to 3 minutes, or until boiling. Remove from oven. Let potpourri stand. When cool, microwave as directed once or twice more.

Dough Art

Create distinctive gift tags or decorate an old-fashioned family Christmas tree with ornaments made in the microwave.

Ornament Dough

- 3 cups all-purpose flour
- ¾ cup salt
- ¾ teaspoon powdered alum
- 1¼ cups water

In large mixing bowl, combine flour, salt and alum. Mix well. Add water. Mix well and shape dough into ball. Knead dough on lightly floured surface for about 5 minutes, or until smooth. If dough is too stiff, sprinkle with water; if too moist, add flour. Work with small portions at a time. Store excess dough in airtight container.

Form shapes as desired (pages 142 and 143). Decorate cutouts with bits of dough in the shape of leaves or bows. Use a drinking straw to cut hole, ¼-inch or larger, near top of cutout for hanging or for tying to gift. Microwave as directed, page 142, for the amount of time specified in the chart, page 143.

How to Microwave Ornament Dough

Spray 10-inch pie plate with vegetable cooking spray. Prepare ornament dough, page 140. Place ornaments in prepared pie plate.

Microwave at 30% (Medium Low) as directed in chart opposite, or until tops of ornaments feel dry, rotating plate and checking ornaments every 2 minutes.

Remove ornaments to cooling rack. Set aside for 24 hours to complete drying. Paint with water colors or acrylic colors.

Cookie Cutter Ornaments

Prepare dough as directed, page 140. Roll dough on lightly floured surface to ¼-inch thickness. Dip edges of cutters into vegetable oil. Cut out shapes with 2½ to 4-inch cookie cutters or with pastry cutter. Decorate cutouts or connect several shapes to make one large 5-inch ornament. To connect pieces of dough, moisten with water-dipped paintbrush. Yields forty 2½ to 3-inch ornaments or twenty-four 3½ to 4-inch ornaments.

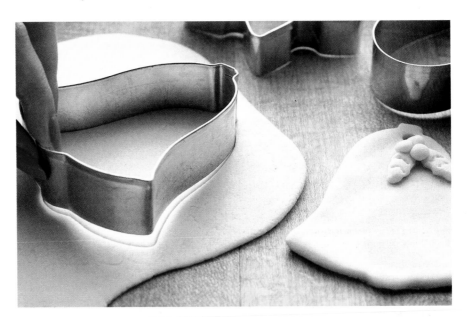

142

Microwave Time Chart for Ornaments

Quantity	Diameter	Microwave Time 30% (Medium Low)
4 cookie cutter ornaments	2½-3-inch	5-10 min.
3 cookie cutter ornaments	3½-4-inch	5-10 min.
1 cookie cutter ornament	5-inch	5-10 min.
2 twisted or braided ornaments		6-10 min.
2 bear ornaments		6-8 min.

Teddy Bear Ornaments

Prepare dough as directed, page 140. Roll dough on lightly floured surface to ¼-inch thickness. Dip edges of cutters into vegetable oil. Cut one 3-inch circle for body, one 2-inch circle for head, and seven 1-inch circles for 4 paws, 2 ears and 1 muzzle. Hand-shape fifteen ¼-inch circles to use for 12 toes on paws, and for eyes and nose. Yields 16 ornaments.

Twisted or Braided Ornaments

Prepare dough as directed, page 140. Hand-roll small pieces of dough into ¼-inch round ropes, each about 8 inches long. Make 2 ropes for twisting, or 3 ropes for braiding. Moisten one end of each rope, and pinch moistened ends together. Twist or braid. Shape into wreath or candy cane. Decorate with small pieces of dough shaped into holly leaves, berries or bows. Yields 16 ornaments.

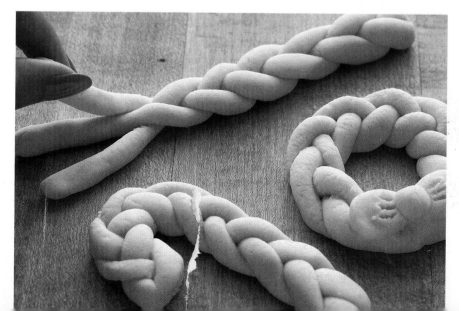

Delight the youngsters and the
young-at-heart with these
charming variations on the
traditional gingerbread house.
Make one building or a whole
village. Use your imagination
to create your own designs.

How to Cut
Graham Cracker Bricks

Cut each whole graham cracker
along perforations to yield 4
bricks, using 8-inch chef's knife.
Patterns call for whole bricks,
three-quarter bricks, half bricks
and quarter bricks. Cut bricks for
desired patterns, pages 148, 150
and 152, before melting mortar.

How to Microwave Mortar

Melt white candy coating ⅛ lb.
(1 square) at a time, because coating hardens as it cools. Melt as
directed in chart, page 107. Spoon
coating into 1-quart sealable
freezer bag. Squeeze coating
to one corner of bag. Seal bag.
Using scissors, snip corner
slightly to form writing tip.

145

How to Assemble Graham Cracker Base

Arrange 10 whole graham crackers on wax-paper-lined baking sheet, ⅛ inch apart in 2 rows of 5. Pipe mortar between graham crackers. Press together slightly. Let stand until set. Set aside.

How to Assemble Walls & Roof Panels

Assemble walls and roof panels, as shown in patterns on pages 148, 150 and 152, by placing bricks ⅛ inch apart on wax-paper-lined baking sheets. Pipe mortar between bricks. Press together slightly. Let stand until set.

Trim tops of end walls as shown in patterns on pages 148, 150 and 152, using 8-inch chef's knife. Decorate roof panels by piping mortar designs or attaching multi-colored fruit-flavored gumdrop slices with mortar.

How to Assemble Buildings

Decorate walls and roof panels before assembling. (See details pages 149, 151 and 153 for decorating ideas.) Place prepared graham cracker base on a piece of sturdy cardboard. Pipe mortar along bottom edge of one side wall. Place on base. Hold in place, or support with heavy object, until set.

Pipe mortar along side and base of adjoining wall. Hold in place several minutes until set. Continue with remaining walls. Pipe additional mortar along edges where walls join. Let stand until set.

How to Make Roof Support

Make supports for church and cottage by piping a heavy line of mortar on the inside of each roof panel, the length of supporting wall. Apply about 1½ inches from bottom for cottage and ½ inch from bottom for church. Let stand until set.

How to Attach Roof

Pipe mortar along top edge and sides of walls. Position decorated roof panels in place, resting piped roof support along top edge of wall. Let stand until set.

Pipe mortar along top of roof where panels meet. Attach round peppermint candies, if desired. Let stand until set.

How to Make Shrubs & Trees

Use 1 large gumdrop for base. Attach small multicolored gumdrops to base, using colored wooden picks. (Break picks to desired lengths.) Decorate sugar cones as directed, page 122, for trees. Place next to buildings.

How to Make Village People

Use round peppermint candies for faces. Use mortar to attach silver balls for eyes and small pieces of shoestring licorice for mouth. To make hair, press one large gumdrop through a garlic press. Style hair and shape around face. (Hair will be sticky, but hardens when exposed to air.)

Cut sugar cone about 2 inches from pointed end, using serrated knife. Trim pointed end slightly to flatten. Discard large end. Using mortar, attach head to small end of body. Hold in place until mortar begins to set. Allow mortar to set before decorating body.

Pipe mortar onto body to make clothing. Before mortar sets, decorate with colored sugar and multicolored shot. Pipe mortar to make arms. Flatten large gumdrops and cut small pieces to make muff, scarf and belt buckle.

Graham Cracker Cottage

What you will need:

28 whole graham crackers
About 1½ lbs. white candy
  coating
Several 1-qt. sealable freezer
  bags
Multicolored hard candies
Multicolored fruit-flavored
  gumdrop slices

Fruit-flavored bite-size candies
Red licorice
Red shoestring licorice
Red cinnamon candies
Round peppermint candies
Green gumdrop wreaths
Silver balls
Large multicolored gumdrops

Small multicolored gumdrops
Red and green colored sugar
Cream-filled wafer cookies
  (2½-inch)
Multicolored candy-coated
  licorice pieces
Multicolored shot

Cottage Pattern   Assemble base, walls and roof panels as directed in Village Basics, pages 146 and 147.

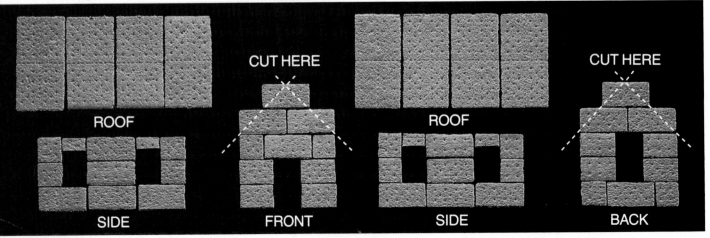

ROOF

CUT HERE

ROOF

CUT HERE

SIDE   FRONT   SIDE   BACK

Cottage Details   Follow directions for details or choose details from other village buildings.

How to Decorate Windows

Fill windows with multicolored hard candies. Pipe mortar around candy pieces to make windowpanes.

Pipe mortar over cream-filled wafer cookies in crosshatch design. Sprinkle with multicolored shot. Use mortar to attach shutters, and attach pieces of licorice for flower boxes.

How to Make Icicles

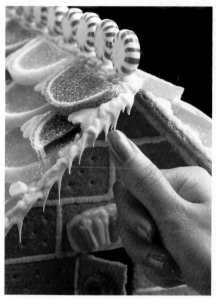

Pipe mortar heavily along edge of roof. Touch with thumb and pull down slightly to form icicles. Let stand until set.

How to Make Door

Use 1 brick for door. Use mortar to attach hard round candy to door for wreath. Tie shoestring licorice into bow, and use mortar to attach below wreath. Pipe dot of mortar for handle, and attach silver ball. Let stand until set.

Pipe mortar down one long side of door; attach to door frame. Hold in place until mortar begins to set. Let stand until set.

How to Make Sidewalk

Pipe mortar in 2-inch-wide strip from front of door to edge of base. Place hard round peppermint candies in mortar for stones. Use red cinnamon candies to fill in between stones.

Graham Cracker General Store

What you will need:

28 whole graham crackers
About 1½ lbs. white candy coating
Several 1-qt. sealable freezer bags
Multicolored candy-coated licorice pieces
Cream-filled wafer cookies (2½-inch)
Multicolored hard candies
Red hard candies with hole in center
Small candy canes
Large candy cane
Round peppermint candies
Sugar cubes
Red and green gumdrop wreaths
Small multicolored gumdrops
Large multicolored gumdrops
Red shoestring licorice
Silver balls
Red cinnamon candies
Chocolate sandwich cookie
Multicolored fruit-flavored gumdrop slices

Store Pattern Assemble base, walls and roof panels as directed in Village Basics, pages 146 and 147.

CUT HERE

ROOF   FRONT   SIDES   BACK

General Store Details
Follow directions for details or choose details from other village buildings.

How to Decorate Roof

Spread mortar in even layer over top of assembled roof. Place multicolored fruit-flavored gumdrop slices evenly on top of roof. Let stand until set. Attach roof as directed, page 147.

How to Make Awning

Coat the top of 1 brick with mortar. Attach small gumdrop halves, or sprinkle with multicolored sugar. Let stand until set.

Pipe mortar heavily along one edge of awning. Position awning in place above door, piped edge against wall. Support with heavy object, or hold until set. Use mortar to attach 1 candy cane support on each side of awning.

How to Make Lamppost

Cut small hole in top of large gumdrop. Pipe small amount of mortar in hole. Insert curved end of large candy cane in hole. Lay on side until set.

Stack 2 or 3 gumdrop wreaths for lamppost base. Insert straight end of candy cane. Attach lamppost to graham cracker base, using mortar. Hold in place until mortar begins to set.

How to Make Bench

Use 2 cream-filled wafer cookies for bench. Attach back to seat, using mortar. Attach 2 sugar cubes for legs, and candy-coated licorice pieces for arms. Let stand until set. Place on base in front of store.

Graham Cracker Church

What you will need:
33 whole graham
 crackers
About 1 lb. white candy
 coating
Several 1-qt. sealable
 freezer bags
Multicolored candy-
 coated licorice pieces
Multicolored hard
 candies
Large multicolored
 gumdrops
Red shoestring licorice
Multicolored fruit-
 flavored gumdrop
 slices
Small candy canes
Round peppermint
 candies
Multicolored shot
Round flat gumdrops

Church Pattern Assemble base, walls and roof panels as directed in Village Basics, pages 146 and 147.

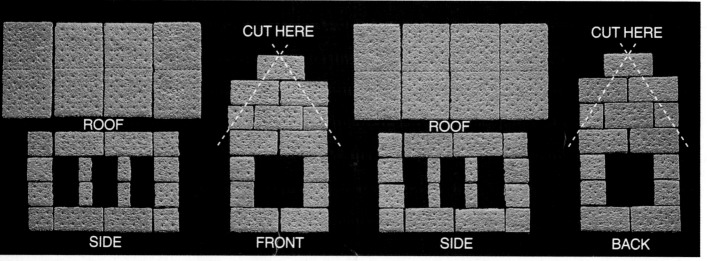

ROOF CUT HERE
SIDE FRONT

ROOF CUT HERE
SIDE BACK

Church Details
Follow directions for details or choose details from other village buildings.

How to Make Stained Glass Windows

Fill windows with multicolored hard candies. Using mortar, fill in spaces around candies. Cut round flat gumdrops in half, and attach one half above each window to make arch. Pipe additional mortar around windows. Use mortar to attach candy cane ledges.

How to Make Steps

Overlap 4 multicolored fruit-flavored gumdrop slices slightly. Attach, using small amounts of mortar. Place round peppermint candies under steps for support. Break candy canes to desired lengths for railings. Attach with mortar. Hold in place until set. Attach doors as directed, page 149.

How to Make Bell

Cut small hole in top of 1 large gumdrop. Pipe small amount of mortar into hole. Insert one end of a 1½-inch piece of shoestring licorice for rope. Let stand until set. Pipe mortar around bottom of gumdrop to make bell. Let stand until set.

How to Make Steeple

Cut 2 whole graham crackers in half crosswise for steeple roof and walls. For steeple roof, hold 2 graham cracker halves at right angle.

Pipe mortar along edge where crackers join. While mortar is still wet, insert rope end of bell in roof seam. Support with heavy object, or hold in place until set.

Use mortar to attach walls. Hold in place until set. Pipe mortar along bottom of steeple walls. Attach steeple to roof. Hold in place until set.

Index